THE BOER WAR

THE BO

Guns Captured
From Boers
At Bothaville
Nov 6 1900

ER WAR

TABITHA JACKSON

First published in 1999 by Channel 4 Books, an imprint of
Macmillan Publishers Ltd, 25 Eccleston Place,
London SW1W 9NF and Basingstoke.

Associated companies throughout the world.
www.macmillan.co.uk

ISBN 0 7522 1702 X

Text © Tabitha Jackson, 1999

9 8 7 6 5 4 3 2 1

A CIP catalogue record for this book is available from the British
Library.

Designed by Roger Hammond
Colour reproduction by Speedscan
Printed in Milan by New Interlitho

TELEVISION

This book accompanies the television series *The Boer War* made
by Twenty Twenty Television for Channel 4.
Executive producer: Claudia Milne
Producer/Director: Jonathan Lewis

Frontispiece: *The Boer General Christiaan de Wet became a folk
hero after a series of daring escapes from the British.*
Title page: *A cursory glance at contemporary photographs gives the
lie to any notion of a 'white man's war'.*
Right: *Although the Boers were considered by the British to be no
more than primitive farmers, their use of the latest rapid-fire
weapons and smokeless ammunition changed the face of warfare in
the twentieth century.*

CONTENTS

INTRODUCTION

THE BOER WAR WAS many wars, and the further we get from it, the more of them we can see. At the time, it was a bitter conflict between two small Boer nations, fighting for their life and freedom, and a great empire asserting what it saw as its legitimate authority. As the century passed, the Boer War came to have very different meanings to these two principal protagonists. It became central to the creation mythology of the Afrikaner nation, whereas nearly 10,000 kilometres to the north it was relegated by two world wars to the very edge of Britain's consciousness.

Now neither these two feisty Boer states, nor that overweening empire, exist. But the Boer War refuses to die. It has an uncanny way of pointing us to issues and emotions in our times – like a vaccination we have refused, only to fall ill with the disease. When people take

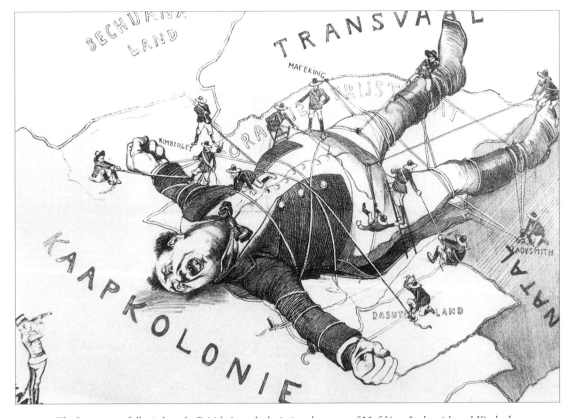

The Boers successfully tied up the British Army by besieging the towns of Mafeking, Ladysmith and Kimberley.

up a fight against a mighty power and turn it into a guerrilla war, look back to the Boer War. When that mighty power finds itself run ragged by people it thought it could squash within weeks, look back to the Boer War. When soldiers advance under creeping artillery fire, or shoot rapid-firing, high-powered rifles from trenches, look back to the Boer War. When civilians have their homes looted and burned and are herded into cattle trucks and packed off to concentration camps, look back to the Boer War. When spin-doctors manipulate the media's war coverage, look back to the Boer War. More civilian losses than military? The Boer War. Both sides riven with internal dissent as to the justness of the cause? The Boer War. The list is as long as the subsequent wars: the Spanish Civil War, both world wars, Vietnam, Kosovo…

Soviet historians used to say that the interesting thing about the past is that you never know what will happen there. A closer look at an unremarkable grassy slope near Alleman's Siding revealed graves: the site of a black concentration camp. Its discovery is the result of co-operation between a local historian, the

The reconnaissance balloon was an innovative if underused addition to the British army.

landowner and a black farm worker. The Boer War's capacity to surprise us, and to make us think and rethink, continues. Now, since Nelson Mandela's remarkable feat of national liberation, we are starting to see the Boer War as an African war. In what sense was it a fight for the freedom of the Afrikaners' land when that land had been taken from the blacks who had been there for thousands of years? How can it have been a white man's war when there were more blacks under arms at its close than there were Boers active in the field? What promises – explicit or implicit – were made to the blacks to win their support, and why did they go unfulfilled?

Tabitha Jackson's timely re-examination, like the Channel 4 series it accompanies, sees it as many wars, yet bound by a complex of linking threads into one. She sees it as a British, Boer and black conflict. She doesn't shy away from the uncomfortable or the distressing. We come to see the war's paradoxes as complementary: as all part of the same bloody and divisive mass. This book could not have been written ten, or even five, years ago. That is what makes it and the war it describes so fascinating.

JONATHAN LEWIS

*A small group of burghers originally sent to southern Africa
by the Dutch East India Company formed a new race of
people – the Afrikaners.*

CHAPTER ONE

All God's Children

If there be a God, I think that what he would like me to do is to paint as much of Africa British-red as possible and to do what I can elsewhere to promote the unity and extend the influence of the English-speaking race.

CECIL RHODES

The Boer people felt that the Lord led them so far, and they had a right to the land. They had given their belongings and their blood for this country, and they had a right to this land.

ROSE VAN RENSBURG

WHEN JAN VAN RIEBEECK was sent by the Dutch East India Company to establish a provision-station at the Cape of Good Hope, little did he realize that he was also establishing a new race of people. It was 1652, and the ships sailing the profitable spice-route to the East Indies needed a stopping-off point where they could take on supplies of fresh meat and vegetables for their scurvy-ridden sailors. All that was required was a fort and a productive garden. There was no intention to colonize this southernmost tip of Africa, and the Company specified that the settlers were allowed only minimal contact with the indigenous Khoikhois in order to trade for their cattle. By 1655, though, the fort had still not been completed. There had been a succession of crop failures, and Van Riebeeck warned the Company that the mission would fail unless some of the Company's servants were allowed to become 'free burghers' with their own farms. The wage bill would be reduced, and fresh produce would be provided at a preferential rate.

So in 1657 nine burghers were given letters of freedom and settled on land close to the fort. But one man's homestead was another man's traditional grazing land, and the Khoikhois were not about to give it up without a fight. Only five years after arriving without any expansionist intentions, Van Riebeeck established the principle of the right of conquest, and the Khoikhois were dispossessed of their grazing rights. Not long afterwards, the free burghers got a taste for liberty and finally escaped the influence of the Dutch East India Company altogether by moving further inland. 1658 was also the year in which the first slaves were introduced to the Cape. By 1707 a census would record 1,779 settlers, owning 1,107 slaves.

Within only a few years a new people had developed. They called themselves Afrikaners and spoke a creolized form of Dutch: Afrikaans.

Two kinds of Afrikaner male had already emerged: there was the settler who remained near Cape Town, growing wheat or making wine. He was relatively affluent, socialized and educated. Then there was the Trekboer (migrant farmer), the wandering pastoralist, who was so geographically and spiritually isolated that his line could only be sustained through intermarriage. He was an individualist whose main comforts in his lonely frontier existence were the teachings of the Dutch Calvinist Church. He was like an Old Testament patriarch. He felt himself to be one of the Elect of God, innately superior to the natives – the 'kaffirs' – he surrounded himself with to perform the necessary hard manual labour. From this brand of Afrikaner came the group that was to give the British so much trouble.

India was the jewel in the British Empire's crown, and in order to protect the vital sea route for its own lucrative spice-trade Britain, too, need-ed the Cape of Good Hope. By 1820 the British had seized the opportunity to annex the cape from the Dutch and had imported 5,000 settlers in an attempt to stabilize the frontiers of the eastern cape. There was increasing hostility between the Trekboers moving east and the Africans moving west. They were both looking for cattle and land and there was not enough to go around.

With these three sets of players – English-speakers, Afrikaners and black Africans – the stage was set for centuries of bloody territorial disputes to determine whose South Africa it was.

The increasing interference by the authorities of Cape Colony in the lives of the Afrikaners, and in particular their liberalizing tendencies towards the rights of blacks, brought about a defining event in the construction of the Afrikaner national identity. In 1834 slavery was abolished. This was the last straw for many of the Afrikaners who depended on slaves for the 'kaffir work' that they felt was beneath them. From 1836 to the early 1840s, between 12,000 and 14,000 Voortrekkers (early migrants) made the Great Trek north from Cape Colony in search of new land and self-determination.

Having crossed the Orange River, they split into two groups. One group went north into the Transvaal; the other headed east towards Natal. This second group, although managing to evade the Xhosa, came face to face with the formidable martial force of the Zulus. The Voortrekker leader Piet Retief decided to try to negotiate land-settlement with Dingaan, the Zulu chief, and even got as far as signing a treaty. But when Dingaan held a gathering to celebrate the signing, on 8 February 1838 he arranged for Retief and his men to be killed. He also sent his men to the main Boer encampment where they butchered 281 Boer men, women and children and 200 coloured (mixed race) servants.

A Boer commando was mustered, intent on revenge, and they gathered on the edge of the Ncome River to prepare themselves both spiritually and strategically. This included sixty armed blacks brought along by an Englishman. They were aware of the scale of the task ahead of them and, there in the middle of Zululand on the Sunday before going into battle, the Vow of the Covenant was sworn. One of the trekkers, Sarel Cilliers, climbed on to a gun carriage and his words passed into Afrikaner legend:

> ...at this moment we stand before the holy God of heaven and earth to make a promise, if He will be with us and protect us and deliver the enemy into our hands so that we may triumph over him, that we shall observe the day and the date as an anniversary in each year and a day of thanksgiving like the Sabbath, in His honour...

On the morning of 16 December 1838 the only thing standing between 530 Boer marksmen and 10,000 Zulu warriors was a circle of wagons. But at the end of an unrelenting assault by the spear-wielding Zulus, only three Boers were injured. It was proof, if any were needed, that God had favoured the Afrikaners. 3,000 Zulu warriors lay dead, and the Ncome ran red with their blood. The Battle of Blood River, as it came to be known, had a profound effect on the Afrikaners' perception of themselves as a 'chosen people'. Manie Maritz, whose father was to make a name for himself in the Boer War, still feels its significance today:

> I think that the Afrikaner was born at the Battle of Blood River...Many researchers say that it was a miracle of God that that battle could have been won then. So we say that that was the birth of this people...And those same people moved in and declared the Transvaal as their own land, the Free State as their own land, and the north of Natal as their own land,

with the full knowledge of the world. It's not like we did it without them knowing about it.

But the Boers' territorial gains were short-lived because the British wanted the vital sea port of Durban and annexed Natal in 1842. There was an uneasy truce, though, when in 1852 and 1854 Britain agreed to recognize the independence of the two Boer Republics of the Transvaal and Orange Free State (later called the Zuid Afrika Republik, or ZAR).

Meanwhile, the territorial disputes between the British and the black South Africans continued. In 1847 the seventh frontier war between the English-speaking settlers and the Xhosa prompted the colonial forces to implement a scorched-earth policy. The local newspaper made its views clear:

> Let war be made against Kaffir huts and gardens. Let all these be burned down and destroyed. Let there be no ploughing, sowing or reaping. Or, if you cannot conveniently, or without bloodshed prevent the cultivation of the ground, take care to destroy the enemy's crops before they are ripe, and shoot all who resist. Shoot their cattle too wherever you see any. Tell them that the time has come for the white man to show his mastery over them.

Just over fifty years later, an almost identical policy would cause questions to be asked in the House of Commons. The difference was that in 1901 the scorched-earth policy was being used against white people.

The situation may well have carried on like this – containable skirmishes and frontier scuffles – had it not been for two chance discoveries that would direct the course of South African history and underpin the reasons for war in 1899.

One day in 1867, quite by accident, a man saw some children playing with shiny stones near the

Orange River. This simple observation was to result in an influx of several thousand people attempting to make their fortunes from the alluvial deposits along the Orange, Vaal and Harts Rivers. What really caught the world's attention, though, was the discovery three years later of diamond-bearing rock on a farm belonging to a man called Johannes Nicolaas de Beer. It was the possibility offered by these dry diggings which caused a large-scale rush, and by 1871, 50,000 people were all living in a mining town that was to be named after the colonial secretary, the first Earl of Kimberley.

Diamond digging at Kimberley quickly moved from individual black and white diggers mining small claims by hand to a more centralized mining industry. Companies now employed large numbers of African migrant workers, who could be paid less than the white miners and were housed in large compounds covered with wire netting.

Above: The Battle of Blood River is now seen as a defining moment in the creation of the Afrikaner identity.
Opposite: The discovery of diamonds at Kimberley in 1867 began the mineral revolution and subsequent industrialization of southern Africa.

With centralization came mechanization, and Johannes de Beer's farm, which he had sold almost immediately, became the site of the world's largest man-made hole, measuring 1.5 kilometres in circumference. The Victorian writer Anthony Trollope visited Kimberley in 1877 and wrote of the enormity of this open-cast mine, known as the Big Hole, in his book *South Africa*:

> It is as though you were looking into a vast bowl, the sides of which are as smooth as should be the sides of a bowl, while round the bottom are various marvellous incrustations among which ants are working with the usual energy of the ant-tribe...

When the world below is busy there are about 3,000 Kaffirs at work...The task is to pick up the earth and shovel it into the buckets and iron receptacles... You look down and see the swarm of black ants busy at every hole and corner with their picks moving and shovelling the loose blue soil.

A new class of mining capitalist was born, headed by the Englishman Cecil John Rhodes, a staunch imperialist with an implausibly high voice. By 1889 De Beers Consolidated Mines, under Rhodes' control, had succeeded in buying up all the other Kimberley mining compa-

By 1891 Cecil Rhodes controlled a company that owned ninety per cent of the world's production of diamonds.

nies, and by 1891 Rhodes was responsible for ninety per cent of the world's production of diamonds.

Although Rhodes controlled the mines, the question of who owned the land around them was by no means clear-cut. Each of the Boer republics claimed that the land was theirs; so did the chiefs of the Tswana people, and so did Nicholas Waterboer on behalf of the western Griqua (a mixed-race people descended from whites and Khoikhois). Britain, taking a not altogether disinterested role, appointed the Lieutenant-Governor of Natal to lead a commission to decide the issue. He found in favour of Waterboer, who promptly asked for protection against his Boer rivals. Thus, the diamond fields of Kimberley were annexed by the British and incorporated shortly afterwards into the Cape Colony.

While the discovery of diamonds was important in itself, it also acted as an instructive foretaste of what would happen when gold was discovered less than twenty years later. Capitalists, the same ones in fact who had made their names in Kimberley, would swiftly move in to industrialize, centralize and attempt to monopolize the mines; the workforce would be structured along racial lines, with black Africans being pulled off the land to perform the hardest work for the lowest pay; and the rights to the land would be disputed. But this time it would take more than a commission to secure the gold-fields for the British Empire.

In 1886 an Australian prospector, George Harrison, came across an outcrop of gold on a farm on the Witwatersrand about 65 kilometres south of Pretoria. Although he didn't realize it, he had just discovered the location of a belt of gold-bearing reefs nearly 50 kilometres long. As the influx of hopeful prospectors began, the Transvaal government sent Christiaan Johannes Joubert and Deputy Surveyor-General Johann Rissik to select an appropriate site for a new city. The city would be called Johannesburg.

The scale of the Witwatersrand reefs made them the biggest known gold-fields in the world, and thousands of people arrived in South Africa to make their fortunes. Australians, Canadians, and German, Cornish and Welsh miners joined destitute Afrikaners and Africans from throughout southern Africa. By 1896 there would be 100,000 people all living together in what one observer described as 'Monte Carlo imposed on Sodom and Gomorrah'.

Although the reefs were vast, the quality of the gold deposits was of disappointingly low grade,

Below and opposite: The gold reefs transformed the Transvaal into 'one of the richest spots on God's earth'.

and the layers of gold-bearing rock ran thousands of metres deep. The South African mines would eventually be the deepest in the world, running to depths of 3 kilometres. This meant that the cost of the processes necessary to extract even a small amount of gold ensured that mining quickly passed into the hands of large companies.

By the middle of the 1890s the control of the entire gold industry on the Witwatersrand lay with a handful of enormously powerful mining houses controlled by predominantly European 'Randlords'. Men like Alfred Beit, Barney Barnato and Julius Wernher, still breathless from the industrial revolution in Kimberley, now had millions of pounds of capital and thousands of workers at their disposal.

Because of the high technological costs involved in deep-level mining and the fact that the price of gold was controlled, the only way for the Randlords to ensure a decent profit margin was to keep labour costs to an absolute minimum.

This meant limiting the number of white miners who, because of their skills, scarcity and unionization, commanded relatively high wages. Instead, the Chamber of Mines, which had been formed in 1899 to drive down production costs, set up two major organizations specifically to recruit native labour. Ideally the workforce would be made up of predominantly unskilled African migrants, who would be accommodated cheaply in compounds and whose wages would be pegged as low as possible.

The mineral discoveries of the last half of the nineteenth century brought an industrial revolution to the African subcontinent for which it was completely unprepared. Within the space of twenty years South Africa was catapulted from being a pre-industrial economic backwater to a country producing one-fifth of the world's gold output and nine-tenths of the world's diamonds.

But this transformation of South Africa into what would become the most powerful and

technologically advanced country in modern Africa was founded on the underpayment and mistreatment of the native population. It was under the auspices of Rhodes' De Beers Consolidated Mines Ltd that the original pass laws restricting movement were introduced, and the African workers were confined to huge compounds for the duration of their contracts. By the end of the nineteenth century black mine-workers were sometimes being paid nine times less than their fellow whites.

The economic revolution was accompanied by a similarly dramatic transformation in the population. As land prices soared, a new working class was created. The pastoral and agricultural rhythms of the Transvaal were brutally interrupted as the mines' insatiable appetite for labour and land sucked thousands of men, black and white, off the farms and into the cities. Between 1871 and 1875, 50,000 Africans per year flooded into Griqualand West, the area around Kimberley.

In 1870 the number of whites in southern Africa was probably fewer than 250,000, but by 1891 the figure had shot up to 600,000. The area most affected by this immigration was the Transvaal, or the Zuid Afrika Republik as it was now called. The bitter irony that gold should be discovered in the very place to which the isolationist Boer farmers had trekked in order to escape the interference of industrialized Europe was not lost on the Transvaal President, Paul Kruger. Johannesburg now had the greatest concentration of Europeans on the subcontinent, and there was a very real danger that these foreigners, or 'Uitlanders', if given any power at all could politically emasculate the Afrikaners. 'God's children' had not made the Great Trek for that to happen,

As President of the Transvaal, Paul Kruger was forced to endure thousands of godless foreigners demanding the right to vote in his country.

In this French cartoon, Queen Victoria and Joseph Chamberlain are 'painting the map red' with Boer blood.

and so in 1890 Kruger restricted the Uitlander vote to men who had been resident in the Transvaal for at least fourteen years.

Kruger was already being criticized by the Randlords for failing to stamp out the corruption and inefficiency which they saw standing in the way of their profits. The price of dynamite and the cost of African labour still seemed intolerably high to them. They felt that this man, who still believed that the world was flat, was simply incapable of providing a government sympathetic to 'capitalism, industrialization and progress'. In a sense they were right. Kruger was acutely aware of the threat that Britain's imperialist ambitions posed to his republic's independence. He remembered the first Anglo-Boer war of 1877 when the Boers successfully revolted against Britain's annexation of the Transvaal. It was difficult to believe that the British would not try to seize power back again now that it was apparent that they had forfeited control of 'the richest spot in the world'.

Cecil Rhodes, having made his name in Kimberley, had become Prime Minister of the Cape Colony. He made no bones about his imperialism:

> I contend that we are the finest race in the world, and that the more of the world we inhabit, the better it is for the human race. Just fancy, those parts that are at present inhabited by the most despicable specimens of human beings, what an alteration there would be if they were brought under Anglo-Saxon influence.

The British Empire already sprawled across both hemispheres, earning for itself the sobriquet 'the Empire on which the sun never sets'. At its peak it extended over one-fifth of the world's land area and cast its shadow across a quarter of the world's population. Even schoolchildren like eight-year-old Arthur Whitlock growing up in London had a sense of its scale:

> If you were to take any school maps at that time you'd find the predominant colour there was red, a pinkish red really, and that covered places like India, Canada, Australia. In fact it more or less covered the greater part of the world.

Rhodes' sentiments found favour in Britain, especially during this phase of 'new imperialism'. At the end of the nineteenth century there was a significant speeding up of colonial acquisition accompanied by a proliferation of colonial powers like Germany, Belgium and Holland. There were more countries wanting more land. In this climate it was doubly important that Great Britain should consolidate and protect its own Empire while precluding other nations from expanding theirs. It was the expansionist tendencies of Germany in particular that worried Britain. A large slice of south-west Africa had just been annexed by Kaiser Wilhelm II, and there was a significant German Uitlander presence in Johannesburg. At a dinner in honour of the Kaiser's birthday, Kruger had gone out of his way to encourage closer relations:

> Just as a child seeks support from his parents, so shall the young Transvaal state seek, and hopefully find, protection from its strong and mighty motherland, and its glorious dynasty.

Cecil Rhodes' dream of painting the map red involved building a railway from Cape Town to Cairo and joining together the Boer republics and British colonies – federating all southern Africa under the British flag – but that was not going to happen for as long as Kruger was controlling the Transvaal. The restriction of the Uitlander franchise five years earlier had made that perfectly clear. But not only was Kruger thwarting Rhodes' aspirations for the Empire, he was also personally costing him money, for as well as diamonds, Rhodes had an enormous stake in the gold-mines. He hatched a plot with his business partner and fellow Randlord, Alfred Beit, and Dr Leander Starr Jameson.

The idea was that 'Dr Jim' would raise an armed force that would support a Uitlander uprising in Johannesburg to overthrow Kruger's government. Any legal niceties could easily be brushed under the imperial carpet.

In August 1895 Rhodes wrote to Beit:

> You might say, 'Oh yes, wait'. But as you know, we will wait too long; and with its marvellous wealth Johannesburg will make South Africa an independent Republic, which you and I do not want.
>
> Now surely Joseph Chamberlain should see all this. He risks nothing; I risk everything; and yet he will not budge an inch to help a big idea which makes England dominant in Africa, in fact gives England the African continent. I wonder again how the English Empire still retains so much of the world.

By December they had managed to persuade even Joseph Chamberlain, the British Colonial Secretary, to support, albeit covertly, their plan.

The Jameson Raid was a complete disaster. The possibility that getting rid of Kruger might leave the way clear for the Union Jack to be hoisted in Pretoria gave the Uitlanders, who included Germans, Americans and Dutch, pause for thought. But it became apparent that the Johannesburg Uitlanders were in no mood to rise up. Despite a telegram from Rhodes informing Jameson of that fact and urging that he postpone the expedition, Jameson, all dressed up, knew where he wanted to go and not having any support at the other end was not going to stop him. On 2 January 1896 Jameson and his 500 men were defeated and captured outside Johannesburg.

In terms of the stated aims of the raid it had been totally ineffectual, but its repercussions were dramatic. Winston Churchill remembered asking the Liberal politician Sir William Harcourt what he thought would happen next:

'My dear Winston,' replied the old Victorian states-man, 'the experiences of a long life have convinced me that nothing ever happens.' Since that moment, it seems to me, nothing has ever ceased happening... I date the beginning of these violent times in our country from the Jameson Raid.

One immediate result of the abortive coup was that Rhodes cut his own political throat. He was forced to resign as Prime Minister of Cape Colony and had to give up his position as head of the Chartered Company, which controlled Rhodesia. Jameson was sent for trial in England and sentenced to fifteen months' imprisonment. Chamberlain, pleading ignorance, narrowly escaped with his career.

The position of Kruger and his Transvaal government was immeasurably strengthened. Loyal Cape Afrikaners who had been persuaded by Rhodes to accept his vision of an Anglo-Boer alliance now suspected Britain of using honeyed words while she waited to seize the Transvaal for herself. The Orange Free State expressed its support for Kruger, and the stirrings of a nascent Afrikaner nationalism could be felt across South Africa.

The raid also had international repercussions. In Germany, Kaiser Wilhelm II could barely contain his glee, and only a day after Jameson's surrender he congratulated the old president on seeing off the raiders:

I express to you my sincere congratulations that without calling on the aid of friendly powers you and your people, by your own energy against the armed bands which have broken into your country as disturbers of the peace, have succeeded in re-establishing peace, and defending the independence of the country against attacks from without.

Despite the illegality of his actions, Jameson was being viewed as a bit of a maverick hero, and news of the Kaiser's communiqué caused a surge of anti-German feeling in Britain. Queen Victoria, the Kaiser's grandmother, was not amused:

My dear William,
...The action of Dr Jameson was, of course, very wrong and unwarranted, but...I think it would have been far better to have said nothing...

Back came a not altogether convincing reply from the man who would lead Germany against Britain in the Great War of 1914–18:

Most Beloved Grandmamma,
Never was the Telegram intended as a step against England or your Government...I was standing up for law, order and obedience to a Sovereign whom I revere and adore.

The ill-fated Jameson Raid of 1895 put Britain and the Transvaal firmly on the road to war.

Chamberlain tried his best to dissociate the intentions of the British government from the impetuousness of the raiders. On 8 May 1896 he made a speech to the House of Commons which would turn out to be strangely prescient:

> A war in South Africa would be one of the most serious wars that could possibly be waged. It would be in that nature of a civil war. It would be a long war, a bitter war, and a costly war…It would leave behind it the embers of a strife which I believe generations would hardly be long enough to extinguish…to go to war with President Kruger in order to force upon him reforms in the internal affairs of his state…would have been a course of action as immoral as it would have been unwise.

Jan Smuts, a future Prime Minister of South Africa would later write: 'The Jameson Raid was the real declaration of war in the Anglo-Boer conflict… [The] aggressors consolidated their alliance…the defenders on the other hand silently and grimly prepared for the inevitable'.

The crucial lesson that the Jameson Raid had taught Paul Kruger was that he was completely unprepared for the inevitable. If the Transvaal was going to fight for its independence, then he was going to have to get some guns. The Transvaal had no standing army, but every burgher was required by law to possess his own rifle and ammunition. The Raid revealed that almost half the burghers did not own rifles, and those who did had antiquated or redundant ones. The ammunition situation was no better: war could have lasted for only about two weeks before the bullets ran out.

Kruger swiftly ordered ten million cartridges and 37,000 of the very latest Mauser rifles from the Krupps factory in Germany. He also built up an artillery corps of heavy guns (Long Toms), field guns and the new one-pounders or Pom-Poms.

Although the Raid had set Britain and the Transvaal on the road to war, it was the arrival of Sir Alfred Milner in 1897 that made the journey so short. As British High Commissioner in southern Africa he would set the tone of the relations between Pretoria and London. Milner was an ardent imperialist and believed that any compromise with Kruger would be a regressive step. What the Empire needed was a new progressive government in the Transvaal sympathetic to capitalism and the Crown. But in May 1898 Milner had to watch as Kruger was re-elected for a fourth presidential term, trouncing his more moderate rival, General Piet Joubert.

Milner knew that securing voting rights for the increasing number of British Uitlanders in the Transvaal was the only way in which Britain could get the foothold she needed to oust Kruger. But the election victory only strengthened Kruger's resolve to keep the Uitlanders in the political wilderness while simultaneously extracting hefty taxes from them. This combination of complete political intransigence backed up by a dangerously efficient rearmament process led Milner to an inescapable conclusion. If Britain was to win the 'great game for the mastery of Africa', there

Paul Kruger was not going to let the British take control of his country by the back door.

would have to be a showdown with President Kruger and it would have to be soon. He wrote to Joseph Chamberlain:

> **There is no way out except reform in the Transvaal or war...I should be inclined to work up to a crisis...by steadily and inflexibly pressing for the redress of substantial wrongs...It means we shall have to fight.**

Although Chamberlain rebuffed Milner's desire to precipitate a crisis, it looked as though Milner might have his way after all when in December 1898 a British Uitlander was shot dead by a ZARP, a South African policeman. The ensuing furore when the ZARP was acquitted of manslaughter resulted in the Uitlanders drawing up a petition to

Queen Victoria appealing for her help in securing the franchise for what was after all a majority of the population in the Transvaal and one that paid a significant proportion of its taxes.

As the Cabinet considered whether to accept the petition, Milner saw an opportunity to ram his message home:

> It is idle to talk of peace and unity in such a state of affairs...The case for intervention is overwhelming...The spectacle of thousands of British subjects kept permanently in the position of helots...does steadily undermine the influence and reputation of Great Britain.

The result was that Chamberlain sent a dispatch to Kruger saying that the Queen could no longer ignore the grievances of her subjects, the Uitlanders.

As war seemed increasingly inevitable, the moderate Prime Minister of the Cape Colony, W.P. Schreiner, suggested that Milner and Kruger met face to face to try to resolve their differences. The Bloemfontein Conference opened on 31 May with Milner determined to see it fail. Even though Kruger finally offered to slash the residency requirements of the Uitlanders from fourteen years to seven, Milner would not do business and demanded five. When he warned Chamberlain that the conference was about to fail. Chamberlain

Sir Alfred Milner, the British High Commissioner, wanted the Transvaal and its gold mines for the British Empire.

President Marthinus Steyn of the Orange Free State was initially reluctant to be dragged into Kruger's war.

cabled: 'I hope you will not break off hastily. Boers do not understand quick decisions...' But it was too late, and the conference had in fact broken up the day before, on 5 June, with a lachrymose Kruger repeating: 'It is our country you want. It is our country you want.'

President Marthinus Steyn of the Orange Free State immediately ordered Mausers and cartridges from Germany, and Milner advised London to send a force to South Africa, perhaps as many as 10,000. But just over a month after the Bloemfontein Conference was aborted, news came that the Volksraad, Kruger's Parliament, had agreed to move substantially towards meeting the Uitlander demands. Chamberlain suggested that a joint inquiry should look at the new proposals, and on 28 July he gained the support of the House of Commons in sanctioning the use of force if Kruger did not yield.

For the next two months it was as though both sides were simply playing for time. But as Kruger offered concessions accompanied by unacceptable conditions, Chamberlain came under increasing pressure from Milner, and the more jingoistic elements of the press, to take positive action. Weapons and ammunition were streaming into the Boer republics through Lourenço Marques (now Maputo), and, by making a show of force now, Chamberlain might pressurize the Boers into backing down. So on 8 September Chamberlain asked the Cabinet to agree to send 10,000 reinforcements to South Africa.

News of the British Cabinet's decision reached South Africa a day later, but President Steyn of the Orange Free State was still convinced that war

Kruger's declaration of war meant that Joseph Chamberlain's own ultimatum could remain safely tucked away.

could be avoided. When Kruger heard on 22 September that the British were also sending an army corps, he decided that he could afford to wait for Steyn no longer and mobilized the Transvaal forces five days later. Steyn was finally persuaded that Chamberlain meant business and mobilized the Free State on 2 October.

By 9 October an ultimatum had been drawn up demanding that the British pull back their troops from the borders of the republics and send home the reinforcements. Failure to comply within forty-eight hours would be taken as a formal declaration of war.

Chamberlain could not believe his luck. On receiving the ultimatum in the small hours of 10 October, he exclaimed: 'They have done it!' What they had done was to give Chamberlain the perfect public justification for going to war without having to issue an ultimatum of his own.

The tone of the editorial in the following morning's *Daily Telegraph* was unequivocal: 'Mr Kruger has asked for war, and war he must have.'

By the end of the war 440,000 British and
Empire troops had been sent to subdue an army which
never numbered more than about 35,000 at any
one time.

CHAPTER TWO

White Man's War?

To the God of our fathers we humbly entrust the justness of our cause. He protects justice; he blesses our arms; under his banner we march to battle for freedom and for Fatherland.

MANIFESTO ISSUED BY THE BOER REPUBLICS AT THE OUTBREAK OF WAR

The Boers are fighting for everything a man holds dear. They are fighting against a machine soldier. The Boer soldier is fighting for a prize worth winning; Tommy Atkins is fighting for a shilling a day. Hence the difference.

MR EASTON, OF THE *NEW YORK JOURNAL*

PERHAPS IT WAS BECAUSE everyone believed that President Kruger would, as Rhodes put it, 'bluff up to the cannon's mouth' before capitulating, or perhaps it was because for the last forty-five years the British army had had to fight nothing more taxing than 'small wars against natives'. Whatever the reason, the War Office was singularly unprepared for dispatching what would eventually be the largest army sent abroad in British history.

This Vanity Fair *cartoon shows Kruger in typical pose with his pipe and Bible.*

By the time the ultimatum expired at 5 p.m. on 11 October, the two Boer republics had mobilized 35,000 men, who were massed on the borders of Cape Colony and Natal. The British, however, had fewer than 20,000 troops in South Africa. 10,000 of them had hastily been pulled out of India and had arrived just in the nick of time on 7 October. Under the command of Lieutenant-General Sir George White, they were sent out to join the 4,000 troops already garrisoned under Major-General Sir William Penn Symons at the main military depot at Ladysmith. Their role would be to protect Natal and quite literally hold the fort until the main British army corps arrived.

General Sir Redvers Buller was the man chosen to lead the British force to South Africa, but it was by now apparent that he would not be able to get there until November. The ships that were to take his men would not be ready to leave Great Britain before 20 October, and then there was the journey of almost 10,000 kilometres to Cape Town.

All around the country regular troops and reservists were preparing to 'teach those Dutch farmers a lesson'. Minnie Way was a little girl in Scotland and still remembers October 1899:

> I saw the troops coming down from Maryhill barracks, sitting on lorries. They had two long seats back to back and they were singing 'We're Soldiers of the Queen'. That was Queen Victoria. She was a good queen, the old Queen Victoria, and they were going down to the pier in Glasgow to embark for South Africa.

In London, the *Daily Mail* was on hand to describe the scenes as the Guards boarded the trains for the coast:

> Even total strangers, carried away by the enthusiasm, broke into the ranks and insisted on carrying rifles, kitbags…and at Waterloo all semblance of military order had disappeared. The police were swept aside

and men were borne, in many cases, shoulder high…while others struggled through in single file.

Emotional scenes were being played out wherever there were departing troops.

Private Thomas Cook was in the Somerset Light Infantry. He noted in his diary:

> There was a lot of hand-shaking, lovers sighing and mothers crying & wives with their children clinging all around them as they saw their Father going out to the War. Till at last the anchor weighed & off we went amidst cheering of the crowds…

In South Africa, John Moody Lane was reluctantly leaving his family. Lane was an Irishman who had become a citizen of the Transvaal. When war broke out he found himself required to fight on the 'wrong' side. The sight and sounds as he boarded his train were no different from those at Southampton. He recorded them in his diary:

> Great crowd singing 'Volkslied' and 'Being a Free People'…Clergymen and others haranguing the departing warriors, Transvaal colours flying in the air. Wives clinging to husbands, brothers and sisters, sweethearts all waving farewell, tears flowing, excitement at full pitch. I hear an old 'tante' in the midst of her tears, saying to her husband, 'Ach, Hans, bring home to me a small Englishman'…Train starts, amid tremendous excitement, guns being fired all over the show, and we are gone to face the 'British lion' and fight (as they say) for our Independence!!!

Although the War Office in Britain was not as well equipped as it should have been, the sight that met the Transvaal burgher Roland Schikkerling as he

The British army did not expect to be detained long by a force without any parade-ground discipline or even a uniform.

followed his comrades to the borders would have soon put their minds at ease:

> The wagons transporting our impedimenta descended through the pass in a long file…Our vehicles presented a strange spectacle – laundry wagons, grocers' wagons, butchers' carts, trolleys and spiders, many of them bearing the names of the firms or persons from whom they had been commandeered. Irregularly, alongside and between, on horseback and on foot, came the men, each one dressed for war according to his own sweet fancy.

It seemed inconceivable to the British public, and indeed to the British army, that this ragged band of Bible-wielding farmers could hold out for long against the might of Her Majesty's troops. The phrase 'It will all be over by Christmas' soon gained popular currency but proved to be as over-optimistic as it was when it was used just fifteen years later in 1914.

Conscription was not introduced until 1916, and the British army in 1899 was heavily dependent on reservists and volunteers to supplement the small regular army. It is difficult to know whether the men who joined up had a clear sense of what they were fighting for. Did they feel impelled to go to war to protect the honour of the British Empire, or was it a spirit of adventure that took them to the other side of the world? During a presentation shortly before they left England, the Mayor of Totnes in Devon told the volunteers:

[You are] going to repel the invader, and to raise again the old flag of England – banner of England's might – over the Queen's dominions in South Africa [applause] and to restore equal rights between man and man – between black man and white man.

The British soldier was colloquially known as Tommy Atkins, as here in a postcard from the Patriotic Postcard Company of London.

There had been reports concerning the subjugation of black Africans in the Transvaal filtering back from the missionaries in South Africa, and Joseph Chamberlain had gone out of his way to draw attention to it as a means of justifying the war. In October 1899 he told the House of Commons: 'The treatment of natives has been disgraceful; it has been brutal; it has been unworthy of a civilized power.'

The implication was that if Britain was in charge, administering the Transvaal would be handled in a more civilized manner, as was the case in the Cape Colony and Natal. Blacks would, for example, be able to walk on the pavements – a privilege so far denied them by the Boers. They might even have a limited franchise extended to them. In the Cape, the franchise had been extended to any

adult male, whatever his colour, subject to a literacy test and a certain level of income. This may have been an important political cause to espouse, but for a great many people in Britain the 'native question' was not one that was frequently asked. To Mary Liverseed, a young girl in the north of England:

Oh, they were just niggers. We had nothing against them, but they were niggers, and we used to say, 'Eeny meeny miney mo, catch a nigger by the toe. If he squeals let him go, eeny meeny miney mo'.

But this war was about to take place in a country whose population was made up of four million Africans compared with only one million whites. While the question of natives as victims might help to justify the war, the possibility of natives as combatants could jeopardize the position of both sides.

Both the British government and the governments of the Boer republics tacitly agreed that this was to be a white man's war. Despite the offer of thousands of colonial troops from India, East and West Africa and Egypt, the British decided that it would be more prudent to use only 'white' troops from colonies such as Canada, Australia and New Zealand.

Jan Smuts, the State Attorney of the Transvaal, later set out the reasoning behind the Boer decision:

The peculiar position of the small white community in the midst of the very large and rapidly increasing coloured races and the danger which in consequence threatens this small white community and with it civilization itself in South Africa, have led to...a special tacit understanding which forbids the white races to appeal for assistance to the coloured races in their mutual disputes. This understanding is essential to the continued existence of the white community as the ruling class in South Africa, for otherwise the coloured races must become the arbiters in disputes between the whites and in the long run the predominating political factor or 'casting vote' in South Africa. That this would soon cause South Africa to relapse into barbarism must be evident to everybody; and hence the interests of self-preservation no less than the cause of civilization in South Africa demands imperatively that blacks shall not be called in or mixed up with quarrels between the whites. This tacit understanding...[is] the cardinal principle in South African politics.

Smuts' fears were understandable. Whites were significantly outnumbered by blacks in the two Boer republics – there were twice as many blacks as whites in the Orange Free State and ten times as many in the Transvaal. It would not take much to

When the patriarchal Boers went to war, women were expected to become head of the household.

upset the very precariously balanced applecart.

Dorah Ramothibe is now 118. She remembers what life in the Orange Free State was like for her and other Africans before the war:

> You had to crawl on your knees as you went up to the Boer. You had to crawl clapping your hands. You didn't have shoes. You didn't know what shoes were. We saw shoes for the first time when the English came. With the Boers we used to go barefoot.
>
> The boss used to give us a good hiding. He used to beat us women up a lot. He slapped you on the face and threw you to the ground and kicked you with his shoe and then told you to stand up. It was a painful life. Very painful. Very painful.

Such a legacy of ill-treatment could have easily resulted in Africans taking this opportunity of a war between whites to vent their anger. President Marthinus Steyn of the Orange Free State was

particularly concerned about Basutoland. This British-administered self-governing country was home to what one official described as 'the only unbroken tribe of the region'. The Basothos were a relatively wealthy people who could easily raise an armed and mounted force of 30,000 men if they so wished. Given its boundaries with the Orange Free State and also with Cape Colony and Natal, both the British and the Boers were keen that the Basothos should stay out of the war. While the British administrator instructed the chiefs that Basutoland should remain neutral, President Steyn circulated a proclamation:

> Be it known that the English Government have forced a war upon the Transvaal. The real cause of the war is that there are gold-fields and diamonds in the Transvaal which certain English people covet. The Free State is helping the Transvaal in this unjust war that the English Government have brought about. As the Free State is liable to be attacked by the British Government on all sides, it has sent commandos of burghers to the neighbourhood of its several borders in order to defend this country in case of attack. The Free State has stationed such commandos in the neighbourhood of the Basutoland border.
>
> Be it known, however, that the Free State is at peace with the Basutos and has no quarrel with them. No harm will be done to Basutos who remain quiet and take no part in the assistance of the English.

Not all black Africans posed a threat to the Boers; some were even prepared to put themselves at risk to help them. Etienne Mofutsanyana lives in the Orange Free State. His grandfather was faced with a decision at the start of the war and settled on what he saw as the lesser of two evils:

> He used to say that we should never trust the white man, especially the Englishman. You cannot trust them…You cannot even understand what they say.

But the Boer, when he says 'I'll pay you', he really means it. When he says 'I'll beat you', he also means it. The people were told that the English were good people who were Christians. They would stay with them, sit around the table, and eat with them. This is what made the people fight against the Boers – but my own grandfather refused and said, 'I don't know these people, I cannot trust them'. He remained loyal and faithful to the Boers.

As the war progressed and the Boers quickly ran out of supplies, one of the people they came to depend on was Mofutsanyana's grandfather:

> Because the Boers' clothes were torn, my grandfather bought them new ones. He took the horses at night, went to Lesotho, and bought blankets, trousers and all the things they needed…During the night he raised a

During the war thousands of blacks worked alongside the Boers in a non-combatant role.

flag at his house so that the Boers would not get lost. This is how he helped them, until the English heard about this and they arrested him.

The accepted notion of a white man's war did not preclude the Boers from taking their black servants to the front with them. These servants were known as *agterryers*, or after-riders, and boosted the Boer forces by about twenty per cent. The *agterryer* was responsible for the upkeep of the most important thing the Boer possessed – his horse. But Phole Mokoena is under no illusions as to why his father went to war with his white boss or *baas*:

> My father helped Baas Koos Raats during the war because he was his master. Baas Koos Raats was not a person who liked a black person to talk back to him. He wanted to be the one who was in charge. He would say, 'Come with me', and my father couldn't refuse him and say no. We would have to say yes all the time…so my father looked after the horses when they were tired, and he polished the saddles…He also had to carry his gun for him and follow him whenever he was going to fight.

Although the *agterryers* carried guns and ammunition for their masters, they were, strictly speaking, not allowed to use them. But there are documented cases of *agterryers* being armed as Boer numbers dwindled. Fransjohan Pretorius, an expert on the Boer commandos, knows of a case in which a black servant was given an unprecedented say in the military conduct of the commando he was with:

> A fantastic example of a black man who fought on the side of the Boers was that of an *agterryer* named Windvoël, of the Rustenburg commando. The Du Plessis brothers took him along as an *agterryer*, and it soon became apparent that Witvoël was an excellent strategist. And in the guerrilla phase it was he who

Despite its reputation as a 'white man's war', more blacks than Boers were fighting under arms at the end of the war.

made all the suggestions and planned the tactics. The Du Plessis brothers let him have his way, because he said he was fighting for the independence of his country. And he identified with the cause of the Boers.

Whatever the Boers and the British may have thought about the theoretical desirability of fighting a white man's war, it was clearly never going to work in practice – not least because both sides dispensed with the notion when it suited them. This was to be a war fought over the future of South Africa by South Africans. Black Africans had a majority stake in that future.

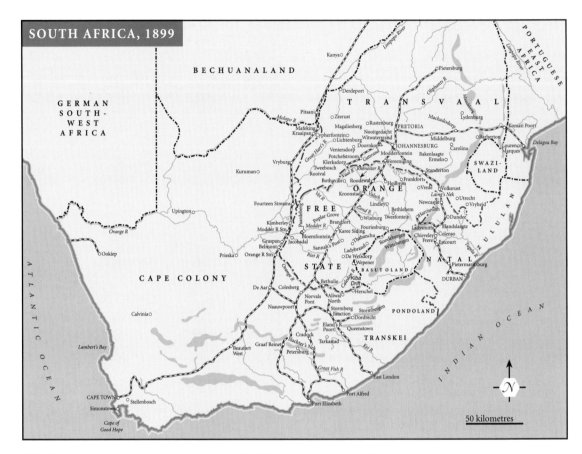

SOUTH AFRICA, 1899

The Boer plan of attack was quite simple. The commandos would effect a swift penetration across the borders of the Transvaal and the Orange Free State into British territory and raise a rebel Afrikaner force in the Cape – all before the British had time to get their main army to South Africa. The idea was to concentrate on four areas: in the west, the area around the British garrisons at Mafeking and Kimberley; in the east, Natal with its British garrison at Ladysmith; and finally in the south, the area around the border of the north-eastern Cape and the southern Orange Free State. As Fransjohan Pretorius puts it:

The idea was to defeat the British garrisons on the borders, and many burghers left with great courage

South Africa in 1899 saw the white population of the Transvaal and Orange Free State surrounded, and significantly outnumbered, by the black population.

with slogans on their hats – 'Cape Town or bust' – or cries like 'We are going to eat bananas in Durban', 'Before Christmas, the war will be over'. That feeling, just like in the first Anglo-Boer War was, that with a few fast, short victories Britain would be willing to give us back our independence.

The first action to be recorded after the expiry of the ultimatum was the capturing of an armoured train at Kraaipan as it carried guns to the British garrison at Mafeking. Although Mafeking was a fairly unremarkable place in itself, it was strategically very important as it held the largest depot on the railway line that led from Kimberley to Bulawayo in Rhodesia. It was also the administrative centre of British Bechuanaland. In July 1899 Colonel Robert Baden-Powell had been plucked from relative obscurity and sent to British Bechuanaland (present-day Botswana) with a mission. His role was to draw off substantial numbers of Boers in the event of war, and thereby reduce the number who would be free to attack the vulnerable areas of Natal and the Cape Colony.

The problem was that Baden-Powell was short of men. As September turned into October, the latest, albeit untrustworthy, intelligence reports indicated that the Boers, poised on the border under the command of General Piet Cronje, numbered anything between 6,000 and 8,000. Baden-Powell (or B-P as he was known) had at his disposal no more than 1,600 armed white men. For him the theoretical desirability of a white man's war was all very well, but when push came to shove he was not about to deny himself an invaluable human resource.

The area around Mafeking was populated by 1,700 whites and 5,000 blacks, a number that

The first action of the war was the Boer capture of an armoured train on its way to Mafeking.

Baden-Powell armed a regiment of blacks to protect Mafeking – a fact he later denied.

swelled to over 7,000 as Shangane mine-boys and homeless Mfengus poured in as refugees. The vast majority of the indigenous black population, though, were Tshidi-Barolong, a Tswana people with a long history of conflict with the Boers. The name 'Mafeking' was taken from the nearby Barolong settlement Mafikeng, meaning 'place of stones'. The white town had been built when Britain had intervened in one of the six previous territorial disputes between the Tshidi-Barolong and the Boers.

Simon Makodi, a Barolong chief, is very clear about the origins of the antagonism between his people and the Boers:

It was because of the land. They wanted to make the blacks slaves and make us work for them. They fought for our land and the money that was being found in this land.

When the Boer came here they found the Barolong people living here in this land. They asked if they could stay for just a while, and the Barolong let them...After that they started to choose land for themselves. They called it their land and not the Barolong's land.

As war became increasingly likely, the Tshidi-Barolong asked for arms and ammunition to protect themselves against the invading Boers. Their requests were repeatedly denied by the resi-dent British magistrate. At an emotional meeting to discuss the issue, one of the Tshidi chiefs was driven to expose an old Boer-inflicted bullet wound on his chest and declare:

> Until you can satisfy me that Her Majesty's white troops are impervious to bullets, I am going to defend my own wife and children. I have got my rifle at home, and all I want is ammunition.

Finally, the Tshidi Chief, Wessels, refused to

GENERAL CRONJE COMMANDO AT MAFEKING 1899

Previous page: *The British army welcomed troops from Australia, Canada and New Zealand, but politely declined any assistance from non-white troops.*

Above: *General Cronje and his men bombarded the inhabitants of Mafeking with the Creusot heavy gun known as the Long Tom.*

provide any of his men for sentry duty in the white town until his demands for arms were met.

So by the time Cronje's men had crossed the border and derailed the armoured train 55 kilometres south of Mafeking, Baden-Powell had assembled and armed a 'regiment' of Barolong

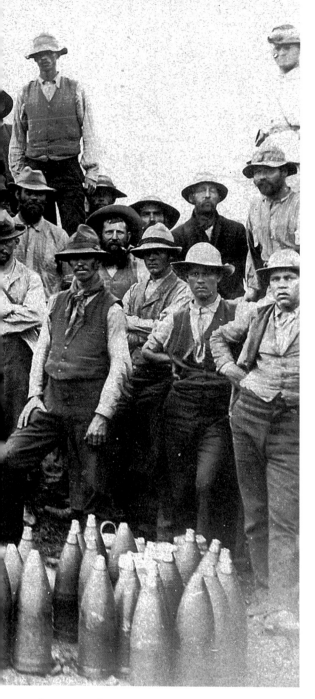

Cronje discovered what Baden-Powell had done he was outraged. He wrote:

> It is understood that you have armed Bastards, Fingos and Barolongs against us. In this you have committed an enormous act of wickedness...You have created a new departure in South African history. It has been a cardinal point in South African ethics, both English and Dutch, to view with horror the idea of arming black against white...reconsider the matter, even if it costs you the loss of Mafeking...disarm your blacks and thereby act the part of a white man in a white man's war.

Cronje was being disingenuous. He himself had reached the outskirts of Mafeking only with the help of the Rapulana-Barolong, traditional allies of the Boers and enemies of the Tshidi. He had used them as scouts and messengers but had also armed them to raid cattle and man the trenches. About 300 Rapulana would take part in the besieging of Mafeking.

One of the last telegraphs that Baden-Powell received before the Boers cut the wires read: 'Whole of England watching you, admiring splendid spirit of you and your garrison.' He displayed the kind of 'pluckiness' the British public loved, and it would make Baden-Powell a national hero.

On 14 October, after a spirited show by B-P's men, Mafeking was surrounded by 6,000 Boers and the siege had begun.

The first shell bombardment scored hits on the hospital and convent – the only two-storey building in the town. Although nobody was killed, it demonstrated how vulnerable Mafeking was. The Boers had bigger and better guns and could remain safely out of the reach of B-P's artillery.

One of the things Baden-Powell was fêted for was his resourcefulness in the face of adversity. Ethne Bernard's mother, who lived in Mafeking during the siege, told her some of the ways in

known as the Black Watch, as well as a coloured contingent from the Cape and a number of Mfengus. He had also put the mine-boys to work on an extensive programme of digging trenches and building siege works to enclose the European town and the native settlement or stad. When

which B-P tried to outwit Cronje's men:

> Baden-Powell was a master of bluff. He had to be because his defenders of Mafeking were very few and they had very little equipment. And one of the stories is of a searchlight that they made out of a biscuit tin which they carried from fort to fort round the town so that the Boers would think that they had lots of searchlights, when in actual fact it was one man legging it from one fort to the other with the biscuit tin. [Also] the defence round their forts wasn't very good so they had the bright idea of putting up barbed-wire fences which didn't exist. They planted some poles and everybody who approached had to step over the 'barbed wire', which they did, solemnly stepping over nothing.

When Cronje brought in an enormous Creusot 94-pounder or Long Tom, which had to be pulled by sixteen oxen, and attempted to blast the town into submission, Baden-Powell's preparations were really put to the test. Fortunately, his system often enabled people like Ethne Bernard's mother to keep out of the way:

> During the siege they evacuated the women and children to a women's laager…When the Boers elevated the big gun, a bell was rung to warn the town that the gun was being elevated…And that was a signal for the children at the women's laager to line up on the veranda to watch for where the shells fell. And they used to run

The diary kept by Sol Plaatje gives a unique insight into a black experience of the siege of Mafeking.

out to pick up the shrapnel. And she said it often burned their fingers.

There was, however, some relief from the fear of where the next shell would drop. Ethne Bernard's mother told her of the one day of the week on which she could relax:

> Well, now, during the siege, as you can imagine, these people were cooped up all the time, but it was a gentleman's war because they had a truce on Sunday; they didn't fight on Sunday. And so on those Sundays they used to have cricket matches at the recreation ground…In the Masonic lodge they used to put on concerts. Now Baden-Powell was very good at that sort of thing, and my mother said that they used to do all of the Gilbert and Sullivan operas.

These regular Sunday pastimes even came to the notice of Sarel Eloff, grandson of Paul Kruger, who was supposed to be making Baden-Powell's life as miserable as possible. The town had been besieged for some months when this letter was found pinned to the railway line outside Mafeking:

> To Colonel Baden-Powell. I see in the *Bulawayo Chronicle* that your men in Mafeking play cricket on Sundays and give concerts and balls on Saturday evenings.
> In case you would allow my men to join in the same it would be very agreeable to me as here outside Mafeking there are seldom any of the fair sex and there can be no merriment without their being present…
> Wishing you a pleasant day,
> I remain your obliging friend
> S. Eloff, Commandant of Johannesburg Commando

Baden-Powell rather stylishly replied:

> Sir, I beg to thank you for your letter of yesterday… I should like nothing better – after the match in which

Although the white inhabitants of Mafeking suffered from the Boer bombardment, the brunt of the shelling fell on the black section of the town.

we are at present engaged is over. But just now we are having our innings and have so far scored 200 days, not out, against the bowling of Cronje, Snijman [Snyman], Botha...and we are having a very enjoyable game.

I remain, yours truly

R. S. S. Baden-Powell

One imagines that there were not very many black faces at the cricket ground or in the audience at the Gilbert and Sullivan recitals. Sol Plaatje was a Barolong interpreter who spoke eight languages and was employed in the local court. He went on to found the African National Congress and his diary brings another dimension to the accepted version of a white-against-white siege. Plaatje preferred to spend his Sundays in church:

> The pulpit was occupied by Mr Lefenya, who warned his hearers to be very careful in their prayers, and remember that their God was the enemy's God. We, however, have the scale in our favour as we have never

raised our little finger in molestation of the Transvaal government, or committed an act that could justify their looting our cattle and shooting our children in the manner they are doing. The weather was fair and shelling and Mausering were conspicuous with their silence. We wished that Sundays would come just a little more often.

For the other six days of the week, civilians were targeted as the two sides tried to wear each other down. The inhabitants of Mafeking, particularly the black ones, were helpless against the random and terrible consequences of the Boer shelling. Despite the fact that they had built the shelters for the whites, blacks were not given materials for shelters of their own. Angus Hamilton, *The Times* correspondent, described the scene just after a shell had burst in the Market Square:

Mingled with the fragments of glass and the contents of the shop were shreds of cloth and infinitesimal strips of flesh, while the entire environment was splashed with blood. The poor native had lost an arm, a foot lay a few yards from him, and his other leg was hanging by a few shreds of skin...When the bleeding body was put upon a stretcher, and the mangled extremities gathered together, the Hospital Orderly caught sight of the hand which was 'clinging' to a recess in the wall...

In the Convent of Mercy, Mother Mary Stanislaus tended to some of the casualties of the shelling:

Often they implored the doctors to take their lives. They tore off the bandages in their frenzy of pain, exposing the maimed limb with its serrated flesh; sometimes gangrened. The odour was often so offensive that those patients had to be isolated.

Eyewitness descriptions such as these give the lie to any perception of the siege as an amusing aside from the main theatre of war. As the shells tore into unarmed civilians, the labelling of the war in South Africa as 'the last of the Gentleman's Wars' also seems strangely inappropriate.

Bloody as the consequences were, Baden-Powell had been successful in his original objective. He had managed to entice one-sixth of the combined Boer forces to Mafeking while they had made no strategic gains whatsoever. Cronje had been effectively stuck in the middle of nowhere for weeks on end.

Neither was the siege good for the morale of the thousands of Boers who were sitting around on the outskirts of Mafeking. A burgher stationed outside Mafeking noted that on one day he smoked his pipe until his mouth was sore, drank coffee until he could hold no more and then told every story he could think of – and after all that it was still only noon. The situation was a stalemate – Cronje did not want to risk the bloodshed involved in a frontal assault on the town, and Baden-Powell did not have the strength to change from a defensive strategy to an offensive one.

After five weeks of being kept at bay by a force seven times smaller than his own, Cronje retired from Mafeking, leaving General J.P. Snyman and 2,000 men to continue to apply the pressure in the only way they knew how. Sol Plaatje recorded the effects in his diary:

The first shell of this morning burst near one of the railway cottages and killed a young fellow by blowing off his belly and pitching his intestines on to the opposite roof. The result of yesterday afternoon's outrage was two whites and a native killed, and two whites wounded. If we are going to die at this rate I am sure there will only be wounded people hopping about single-armed and with amputated legs to tell the history of the siege.

I have never before realized so keenly that I am walking on the brink of a grave...

The Barolongs were not the only Africans to be playing an active role in this 'white man's war'. Like the Barolong, the Ngwato were a Tswana people. They occupied land just over the Transvaal border in Bechuanaland, and King Khama was well known for his loyalty to the British. In the first month of the war he received a pompous letter from the Boer General F.A. Grobler informing him that as he had allowed the British to use his land for 'warlike operations' then Grobler's men would be doing the same. They would not, however, disturb the Ngwato unless the Ngwato actively helped the British. Khama's reply was to the point:

> If you do not intend fighting me, what are you doing in my country with an armed force?
>
> If you enter with armed men into my country, and among my cattle posts, I shall fight you...You must not think you can frighten me, and my people, with your war talk. You know that I am a Son of the White Queen.

Thousands of Ngwato then played a very vital role, helping the British by patrolling the Transvaal–Bechuanaland border, guarding the railway line and getting messages in and out of Mafeking.

Lesobe Phaladi is an elder of the Bakgatlas, whose territory stretched right across British Bechuanaland and over the border into the north-west Transvaal. For them, the war provided an opportunity to settle old scores and reclaim the land they had lost:

> This is our land, the Tswana and other black people. The Boer came and found blacks and the English came and found blacks. We helped because we wanted to get our land back. The land belonged to us.

The Bakgatla in particular had a long history of enmity with the Boers rooted in the forcible appropriation of black land and labour by the whites. In a notorious incident in 1869, the Bakgatla Chief Kgamanyane was publicly flogged by the then Commandant Paul Kruger. This incident and the harsh forced-labour conditions imposed by Boer rule persuaded half the Bakgatla to flee across the Transvaal border and into what would become British Bechuanaland.

> In 1875 Chief Linchwe took over the reign. The whites started coming and they would steal the cattle from the Bakgatla. The Bakgatla people fought with them because of stealing their cattle.

The cattle-raiding that Lesobe Phaladi describes became so provocative throughout the October of 1899 that Chief Linchwe, after some initial politically expedient delays, committed his people to giving their support to the British. They in return provided Linchwe with 6,000 rounds of ammunition, enabling Lesobe Phaladi's grandfather to do a little raiding of his own:

> My grandfather...used to go out at night and steal horses from the Boers, sell them to the English, and give some to the Bakgatla. The English were behind us. They are the ones who gave us the guns, the weapons, because the Boers were busy following us around.

It was not until late November, however, that the Bakgatla's involvement in a British-sponsored raid against the Boers brought international condemnation. The Boers described the collusion as 'the most barbarous [deed] ever committed by a civilized government'.

Colonel G.L. Holdsworth had been appointed to lead a raid on a Boer encampment or laager, at Derdepoort, just inside the Transvaal border. He enlisted the help of three Bakgatla regiments, which were to be led by his British forces. After the British Assistant Commissioner expressed his reservations about using Bakgatlas in military operations in the Transvaal, plans were drawn up to ensure that only Holdsworth's troops would cross the border, leaving Linchwe's men to prevent any Boer incursion into Bechuanaland.

Despite the clear instructions from British High Command and the delicate political situation, Holdsworth changed his mind at the very last moment. As his men stopped for water on the way to Derdepoort a different plan was put into action. Holdsworth was worried that his men's heavy boots would give away their position, so he ordered one of the barefoot Bakgatla regiments to cross the border and take the ground. His troops meanwhile would be led by Segale, Linchwe's half-brother, to a spot from where they could then open fire on the laager.

The next day, 25 November, nothing went to plan. The advance Bakgatla contingent attacked the Boers, but instead of Holdsworth following them up, he did nothing and then completely withdrew his troops, making a speedy exit back across the border.

This action left a regiment of Bagkatla armed, primed and completely at liberty to settle some old scores with the Boers. The result was one dead German, twenty dead Boers, including two

Janice Farquharson's mother (far right) during the siege of Kimberley.

women, and seventeen captured Boer women and children, who were taken back to Bechuanaland along with a hundred head of cattle. The Bakgatlas suffered fourteen dead and sixteen wounded.

It was not clear what had possessed Holdsworth to disregard so flagrantly both the strict instructions of his High Command and the basic principle of conducting a white man's war. He later accused Linchwe's men of disobeying his orders in crossing the border, but there were enough witnesses to prove that this was not the case. Official

A cartoon depiction of Linchwe's men in the front line during the raid on Derdepoort.

Boer sources concluded that the Bakgatla had been forced across the border at the end of a Maxim machine gun, but Lesobe Phaladi is keen that the Bakgatla should not be seen simply as pawns in the Great Game: 'They were fighting according to their free will against the Boers, and no one was forcing them to fight; the English did not force them to fight.'

Whatever the mitigating circumstances, the Boers were swift in their revenge. They carried out bloody reprisals on three border villages, and 150 Bakgatla were killed. But the effects of the Derdepoort Raid also resonated further afield. As details of the incident were made known in Europe, a hostile German periodical published a story alleging that the seventeen women and children who had been taken prisoner had also been gang-raped by both Bakgatla and British soldiers. An investigation concluded that there was no evidence at all to support this, but the damage had been done.

What Derdepoort and Mafeking showed from the very start of the war was that this was to be a struggle for South Africa and that blacks would play just as active a part in that struggle as whites. In fact, only six months later, in June 1900, the Africans of the north-west Transvaal were participating so vigorously in the hostilities that Baden-Powell wrote to the then Commander-in-Chief, Lord Roberts:

> **The Natives are armed and in many places are active in hostility against, and a standing danger to, the Boers. Last week four Boers were wounded and one killed by Natives at different places about the Pilansberg; most of the Boers from that neighbourhood have come to live under our protection.**

On 14 October, the very day that Mafeking was besieged, the same thing had happened 355 kilometres down the western front at Kimberley.

Standing as it did it in Cape Colony, but only six kilometres from the Orange Free State border, Kimberley was an enticing prospect for the Boers. The man in charge of defending an under-protected Kimberley was Colonel R.G. Kekewich and his half-battalion of Loyal North Lancashires. They had a very difficult task ahead of them. Not only would they have constant battles with Cecil Rhodes, who had managed to get back to Kimberley on one of the last trains from Cape Town, but they would also have to be mindful of the fact that about half of the white population of Kimberley was Afrikaner.

Janice Farquharson's mother was a little girl in Kimberly during the siege:

This German picture was captioned 'English princesses decorating the youngest soldier…for having already…raped eight Boer women.'

As far as my family were concerned there would be absolutely no question. Their allegiance...would have been an allegiance to the Queen, and to the idea of empire. And you can laugh at it today, but that is what their feeling was.

Hung round their beautiful bomb-proof shelter, lots of white ensigns...and before the family sat down to a meal, they all stood round the table and sang 'God Save the Queen'.

Kimberley was not subject to the same intensity of shelling as Mafeking. Indeed, one of the distinguishing features of the siege here was that so little happened for such a long time. As Janice Farquharson puts it:

> It would have been very dull, very boring and claustrophobic. I mean, let's face it, I'm born and bred in Kimberley, third generation, but Kimberley is not the most exciting place on God's earth, is it? And I should imagine that with the siege it was possibly even duller.

As the Boer forces bedded down around Mafeking and Kimberley, much of the initial momentum of the commandos was lost. With hindsight it is clear that the Boers should have pressed home their advantages by continuing their advances into British territory rather than skidding to a halt within the first few days of the war. It was a point not lost on Deneys Reitz, who wrote in his account of his experience on commando:

> There was not a man who did not believe we were heading straight for the coast, and it was as well that the future was hidden from us, and that we did not know how strength and enthusiasm were to be frittered away in a meaningless siege, and in the holding of useless positions, when our only salvation lay in rapid advance.

Tommy Atkins would find another enemy in South Africa's extremes of climate.

The first major battles of the war took place in Natal on the eastern front. By the time the ultimatum expired, the limited number of British troops there had been split into two forces. Lieutenant-General Sir George White had stationed 9,600 men at Ladysmith, while Major-General Penn Symons had taken 5,000 men 65 kilometres away to Dundee. Whatever the rights and wrongs of this decision, the inevitable consequence was that the old Boer General Piet Joubert, with 14,000 Transvaal and 6,000 Orange Free State burghers at his disposal, cut off communication between the two towns and sent General Lucas Meyer to deal with Penn Symons. The ensuing battle, which took place on 20 October around Talana Hill, resulted in the British holding on to Dundee but at the cost of 546 casualties, compared with about 150 on the Boer side. In what for many of them would have been their first taste of 'modern' warfare, the British learned the cost of employing the traditional methods of close-order frontal assaults in which the infantry advance packed tightly together, making it easier for a Maxim-wielding enemy to mow them down.

They also learned the limitations of the cavalry when, as the Boers swiftly retreated, the cavalry were nowhere to be seen, and the artillery was too irresolute to scatter the retreating Boers as they fled. Perhaps the most poignant example of the old school was Penn Symons himself. As he strode forwards to encourage his men onward into the enemy fire he exemplified the journalist Donald MacDonald's view of the heroic British officer:

He has no rifle, no cover. With his useless sword in hand he strides bravely on, pointing the way, a conspicuous target for every sharpshooter on the ridge above him. It is the correct thing to do. It is the caste of the officer as compared with the man – and it is magnificent.

It was also, unfortunately, fatal, and Penn Symons was retired, mortally wounded, from the battlefield.

The Boers had cut the communications between Dundee and Ladysmith at a place called Elandslaagte. The day after the battle of Talana Hill, General John French and his Chief of Staff Major Douglas Haig were instructed to retake Elandslaagte, which, by this time, had been occupied by General J.H.M. Kock and 1,000 Boers. French's cavalry was reinforced by 3,000 of Colonel Ian Hamilton's infantrymen. The fighting would take place on Hogsback Ridge, a horseshoe-shaped hill with the Boers occupying one side and the British occupying the other, 5 kilometres away.

After the initial artillery bombardment, the infantry made a frontal assault, this time in open formation with each man over a metre apart from the next. They managed to get to within about 400 metres of the Boers and then stopped to allow a second flank to attack along the curve of the horseshoe. But in a horrible precursor of the Great War, a length of agricultural barbed wire stopped them in their tracks and left them as standing targets for the deadly aim of the Mausers. But Hamilton gathered reinforcements, and the British rallied and overran the crest. Just as it all seemed to be over – some say the Boers had already raised the white flag – General Kock himself came blasting out of nowhere to lead fifty of his men in a devastating counterattack. The British rallied once more and finally took the ridge as the Boers melted away. Unlike at Talana Hill, the 400 Lancers and Dragoons of the cavalry were ready and waiting for their retreating enemy. They caught the Boers by surprise and swept through them in a bloody whirlwind of thrusting lance and hacking sabre in not one but three charges. One officer later summed it up as 'Most excellent pig-sticking...for about ten minutes, the bag being about sixty'.

It was this act that instilled in the Boers a hatred of the British cavalry and a determination, one day, to even the score.

In the last week of October 1899 Colour Sergeant Lee of the First Devon Regiment wrote to his mother about his experiences at Elandslaagte:

No sooner had we come in sight than shells from the enemy's artillery were falling all around us and plenty of poor fellows were killed. On, on we went...and the nearer we got thicker came the bullets and it seemed almost impossible to live...The sights to behold would turn one cold, headless bodies, others disfigured, limbs lying about in all places, for our artillery made grand work on the enemy. I found one poor fellow badly wounded and talking about his poor mother at home and it touched my heart, although he was one of the enemy, I can assure you, for they are white people like ourselves...But still we must be thankful to God for all. We are soldiers and only doing a soldier's duty...This won't be over I am sure for about another four months, as we have got no troops from England yet, and waiting for them badly.

ARMS AND ARMIES

It would be difficult to find two such contrasting armies as those that went to war in October 1899. Apart from the Artillery Corps, the two Boer republics had no standing armies and relied on the mobilization of every man between sixteen and sixty when the time came. There was no uniform, no money and no formal training. All that was required of each burgher was that he had a horse, saddle and bridle; a rifle, plus thirty rounds of ammunition; and enough provisions for eight days. If any of these things were lacking, the government provided them. Unlike Tommy Atkins, as the British soldier was nicknamed, the Boer was often to be seen with a Bible in one hand and a rifle in the other. More than eighty per cent of burghers on commando were members of the Dutch Reformed Church and a common saying was 'If God is for us, who is against us?' The Boer citizen armies were split into commandos of between 500 and 2,000 men who, generally speaking, came from the same area. Their commanding officers were elected by the members of the commando, and all officers, regardless of their rank, had an equal say in war councils.

Such an egalitarian system meant that the Boers did not enforce the kind of military discipline that was so familiar to the British army. To complete the picture of an 'unmilitary' army, the burghers often travelled with their possessions, and their families would pitch their wagons nearby in large encampments known as laagers.

The British army, on the other hand, was strictly hierarchical and spent much of its time drilling on the parade ground. While the Boer army was an army of individuals each acting as he saw fit, the British army was dependent on orders and textbook advances. The Boer in battle would strike quickly, fire quickly and retreat quickly. The British would advance slowly in close order, wait for the command, fire strictly in volleys and then fix bayonets. Whereas the Boers were essentially mounted infantry armed with modern rifles, the proportion of British mounted troops was only about ten per cent. Most of these were cavalrymen dependent on the traditional sabre and lance.

There was a culture of complacency among the British exemplified by the fact that only two intelligence officers looked after the whole of the colonial Empire. The budget for the intelligence division was just £11,000 per annum, compared with the Transvaal's £90,000 per annum. Deficiencies in intelligence would make themselves painfully clear throughout the course of the war. One young bombardier noted in his diary: 'I have heard that, to get a position in the

Even in war the Boer was an individualist. According to Fransjohan Pretorius, 'every Boer was his own general'.

The British army had only recently discarded the traditional scarlet for a more practical khaki.

Intelligence department, one had to prove that he absolutely lacked intelligence.'

The advances in weapons technology in the years leading up to 1899 were vital in determining how this war would be fought. Smokeless powder now meant that a man could fire without giving away his position, and the latest rifles could now rapidly discharge a number of bullets before it was necessary to reload. The Maxim machine gun, introduced in the 1880s, fired for as long as the trigger was squeezed, but, although they  were widely available, the British sent relatively few of these guns to South Africa, believing them to be not quite the thing for 'civilized warfare'. By 1899 naval guns could fire shells up to 32 kilometres, but the more usual type was the horse-drawn field gun that could accurately toss over several kilometres shells weighing between 12 and 15 pounds.

The British would send almost 450,000 soldiers to South Africa in order to defeat a force that never numbered more than about 35,000 at any one time. It was a war that, as Kipling remarked, taught the British 'no end of a lesson'.

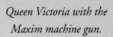

Queen Victoria with the Maxim machine gun.

The Boers inflicted heavy defeats on the British army in the
early stages of the war.

CHAPTER THREE

A Stiff Little Show

I don't think the Boers will have a chance, although I expect there will be one or two stiff little shows here and there...I think they are awful idiots to fight, although we are of course very keen that they should...

LIEUTENANT REGGIE KENTISH, ROYAL IRISH FUSILIERS

If anyone wants to know what war is, tell them it is something like Guy Fawkes' Day up at Hampstead. The only difference is when shells burst up in the air, and instead of coloured fire you get bullets.

LETTER FROM A NINTH LANCER

BY THE TIME THE Commander-in-Chief, General Sir Redvers Buller, landed at Cape Town, things were not looking good for the British in Natal. The previous day, 30 October, had been christened Mournful Monday as the Natal Field Force under Sir George White had met Joubert's men in a series of battles to the north and east of Ladysmith. It was the first time in the war that such large bodies of troops, about 12,000 on each side, had met each other on equal terms. The disastrous result was that the British were unceremoniously pushed back into Ladysmith at the cost of 1,200 men, compared with just 200 on the Boer side. The young burgher Deneys Reitz had fought with the victorious Boers:

Shortly after the surrender I was talking to some of the captured officers when I heard one of them exclaim, 'My God; look there!' and turning round we saw the entire British force that had come out against us on the plain that morning in full retreat to Ladysmith. Great clouds of dust billowed over the veld as the troops withdrew, and the manner of their going had every appearance of a rout…

The British casualty figures could well have been even higher had it not been for Joubert's reluctance to pursue the retreating British.

Sir George White had failed spectacularly in his primary task of protecting Natal until Buller arrived with his invasion force. He had, as a result of Mournful Monday, allowed himself to be besieged in Ladysmith. Buller felt he had no choice but to discard his original invasion plans and to split the army corps into three. He would take the largest force to relieve Ladysmith; Lord Methuen would relieve Kimberley and Mafeking;

and the third force under Lieutenant-General Sir William Gatacre and General French would contain the Boer invasion from the Free State into the Cape until Buller regrouped his forces.

Sailing out with Buller on the SS *Dunottar Castle* had been the young correspondent of the *Morning Post*, Winston Churchill. He was on a record salary of £250 per month plus expenses, and his greatest fear was that all the action would be over before the ship docked at Cape Town. After heading towards Ladysmith in search of some good copy, Churchill found himself caught up in an adventure of his own.

Below: *This photograph shows the exodus from the Transvaal as Uitlanders are crammed into the trucks on to the last train to Natal.*
Opposite: *Winston Churchill's account of his capture and daring escape secured his reputation as an adventurer.*

After sitting around Ladysmith with 22,000 men for two weeks, General Joubert finally gave in to the young General Louis Botha and set up an expeditionary force to prepare for the arrival of Buller's army corps. Botha and his 4,000 men had just swept through Colenso when they had an incredible piece of luck.

At Estcourt, a town between Ladysmith and the capital of Natal, Pietermaritzburg, was a small British garrison. It regularly sent an unaccompanied armoured train to patrol the railway line up to Colenso. Despite knowing that a significant number of Boers were in the vicinity, on 15 November the train was once again sent out, complete with a 7-pound naval gun, 150 soldiers, six plate-layers to repair the line, and Winston Leonard Spencer Churchill.

On noticing the armoured train puffing non- chalantly past them, Botha ordered his men to lay boulders on the line, prepare their artillery and wait for the train to come back. The driver of the train, after hearing the enemy shooting, went full steam ahead and, rounding a corner, hurtled straight into the boulders and neatly into Botha's trap. In one of his dispatches Churchill would say of the enemy:

> **What men they were, these Boers!…Thousands of independent riflemen, thinking for themselves, possessed of beautiful weapons, led with skill, living as they rode without commissariat or transport or ammunition column, moving like the wind…**

He was now able to observe these qualities at close quarters as, after bravely clearing the line and enabling the engine to take the wounded back to

Estcourt, Churchill was taken along with about seventy others as prisoners of war to Pretoria. He recorded his first night in captivity for the faithful readers of the *Morning Post*:

And then above the rainstorm that beat loudly on the cor-rugated iron, I heard the sound of a chant. The Boers were singing their evening psalm, and the menacing notes – more full of indignant war than love and mercy – struck a chill into my heart, so that I thought after all, that the war was unjust, that the Boers were better men than we, that heaven was against us.

For soldiers unused to the terrain, the open veld provided little cover. At Belmont the British had twice as many casualties than the Boers.

With daylight came the return of Churchill's spirits, and he began to look for a way out. It was his daring escape, after being held in the State Model School Prison for almost a month, that secured him a place in the consciousness of the British public, who were anxious for any good news. Before slipping over a wall he left a letter for the Boer Secretary of War, De Souza:

December 10, 1899

Sir,

I have the honour to inform you that as I do not consider that your Government have any right to detain me as a military prisoner, I have decided to escape from your custody. I have every confidence in the arrangements I have made with my friends outside, and I do not therefore expect to have another

opportunity of seeing you. I therefore take this opportunity to observe that I consider your treatment of prisoners is correct and humane, and that I see no grounds for complaint...Regretting that I am unable to bid you a more ceremonious or a personal farewell,

> I have the honour, to be, Sir,
> Your most obedient servant,
> Winston Churchill

With the arrival of Sir Redvers Buller and his plans for a three-pronged assault, the preliminary phase of the war came to an end. The Boers were doing well: they had besieged Mafeking, Kimberley and Ladysmith and had managed to keep all their territory intact while controlling the border districts of the Cape midlands, the northern Cape and northern Natal. The British, while enjoying some success, had sustained heavy losses and had learned several hard tactical lessons. One of those lessons was summed up neatly by an Australian soldier, A.B. Paterson:

> ...But when you're fighting Johnny Boer you have to use your head;
> He don't believe in front attacks or charging at the run,
> He fights you from a kopje with his little Maxim gun.

Major John Buist's father gave him an insight into how complacent his cavalry division were when they first reached South Africa:

> They knew the Boers were virtually farmers without any military training or anything like that and that there wouldn't be very much opposition. And as a result, when the army arrived at South Africa, according to what my father told me, as [there was] very little reconnaissance of where the Boers were located...I remember him saying that...several officers would get together and they'd say: 'See that kopje over there, let's go and see if there's any Boers up there. I'll tell you

what, I'll race you there.' And they'd charge off on their horses and if the Boers happened to be there well then of course they got casualties.

This kind of behaviour would not have lasted for very long. Captain L. March Phillipps was part of a mounted advance party known as Rimington's Guides. He soon formed a different impression of the enemy:

> The Boers, such as I have seen yet, are decidedly awkward-looking customers, crafty, but in deadly earnest, versed in veld wars and knowing the country to an anthill. Looking from one to the other, I fear there are many mothers in England who'll go crying for their boys this campaign.

On 21 November 1899 Lord Methuen began his 120-kilometre march to Kimberley and confidently expected to arrive there within a week. The terrain from Orange River to Kimberley was wide-open plain, the only obstacles being an occasional cluster of hills, or kopjes, and two rivers. Methuen's intention was to follow the railway line and 'put the fear of God' into anyone he should meet on the way.

His first two battles, at Belmont on 23 November and Graspan on 25 November, were, on paper, successes. The British slogged it out with the Boers and managed to take the high ground. But these victories were costly. Inadequate intelligence, poor maps and not enough mounted troops meant that Methuen's casualty figures were almost double those of the Boers. Twice he had had to watch as the losers had been allowed to trot away unhindered, free to regroup for the next encounter.

John Moody Lane, the Irishman reluctantly fighting with the Boers near Kimberley, wrote of how they were not in the least disheartened by the British victories:

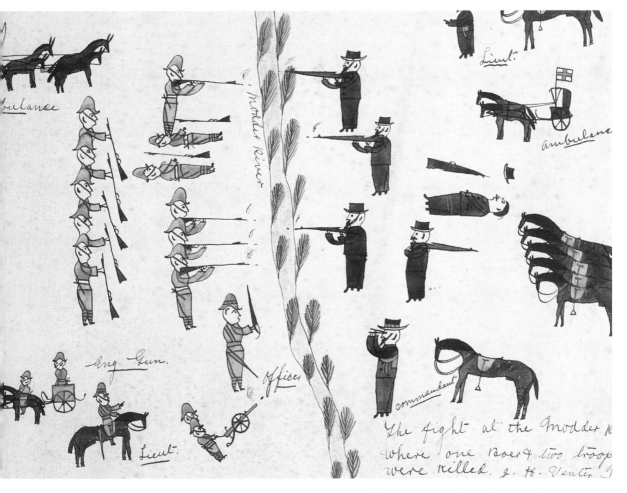

A Boer prisoner of war's simplistic impression of the Battle of Modder River.

In the distance I see a cart coming on, it comes up and I see in it…an old Boer over sixty. [He] stands up in the cart, hat off, and makes a speech to this 'crowd' telling them in thousands of how many British were slain at Graspan and Belmont and he said, 'We are the victors,'…winding up with God gave us the Bible and now he has added the Mauser the British have no chance against us.

But the 'old Boer', as well as hugely inflating the casualty figures, also neglected to mention that after losing at Belmont many Free Staters had returned to their farms. As Manie Maritz, the son of the Boer general, put it:

> If you were a white man in South Africa you had a choice. It was not a professional army. You could choose whether you wanted to plant your corn or if you were going to war.

The Transvaal General, Koos de la Rey, had learned an important tactical lesson: in the last two battles, taking what had seemed to be an

advantageous position on the steep kopjes had led to the Boers' defeat. While giving them a desirable vantage point, it had proved impossible to fire accurately down on the enemy without exposing oneself to their artillery fire. De la Rey decided that the Boers should next meet the British on the level, at Modder River.

His plan was to use the steep banks of the river as a trench. His men would be hidden and, as the unsuspecting British approached without any cover, the Boers could wait until the last moment and mow them down without ever having to show themselves. Cronje was pulled down from Mafeking with reinforcements, along with Commandant Hendryk Prinsloo and his Free Staters. De la Rey made preparations for the daring ambush.

At Modder River, British troops were trapped on the ground in searing heat after the Boers took them completely by surprise.

Lord Methuen, meanwhile, was convinced that the Boers would wait to attack him in the hills near Magersfontein. A frontal attack was the only answer. He wrote to Buller:

We are getting to the bottom of the Boers. It is a mere question of pluck. We are terribly handicapped and I quite understand this country has been the graveyard of many a soldier's reputation. The maps are of little value, the information obtained still less, as the open country plus Mauser rifles render reconnaissance impossible. People talk of making a detour, or sending a Brigade round a flank, there is no use talking that way with 8,000 horsemen in front of you, a river, and a position not to be turned. The job has got to be done.

As Methuen approached the leafy banks of the Modder River on 28 November, he became increasingly sure that the Boers would not try to tackle him there. He ignored the white-painted stones placed carefully to give a ranging point to Boer gunners and even downplayed the importance of reports warning him of Boer presence. As he came within a kilometre of the river banks bristling with thousands of eager Boers, he said to one of his officers: 'They are not here.' The officer presciently replied: 'They are sitting uncommonly tight if they are, sir.'

The Boers could not hold themselves back any longer and let loose on the British a fusillade that one newspaper correspondent described as 'like the ripping of air, like the tearing of some part of nature'. If the Boers had been able to restrain themselves and waited a little longer, the ambush would have been a complete massacre. Totally surprised and with no cover whatsoever, the British dived to the ground. There was nothing to be done. They could neither advance nor retreat. Men lay for ten hours in temperatures that reached 108 degrees Fahrenheit. With no food and no water, some tried to reach the water wagons. They were picked off one by one. The Scots Guards lay flat on their stomachs as the ants crawled all over them, the sun blistered the backs of their legs, and the slightest breeze rippling their kilts gave away their position and brought down another hail of bullets from the invisible enemy. By the time night fell, 500

were dead and Methuen's men had advanced not one metre.

Under cover of darkness the British made plans to reinforce their position, but there was no need. As dawn broke, the Boers had gone, leaving only the bloody aftermath of the night before. L. March Phillipps was there:

Bodies, still unburied, lay about when I was there. Such odours! Such sights! The unimaginable things that the force of shot and shell can do to poor, soft, human flesh. I saw soldiers who had helped to do the work turn from those trenches shaking.

Lord Methuen had lost 1,000 men in his last three battles, but the British public barely had time to reflect on this before they received news of a series of humiliations on each one of Buller's three fronts. Coming as they did within the space of five days, the week beginning 10 December was christened Black Week.

The first disaster was down in the Cape, where the Boers had penetrated the Cape Colony and successfully taken Stormberg Junction. This was a major source of concern to the British because there was a very real chance that the Boers could foment rebellion among the Cape Afrikaners on an impossibly wide front. General Sir William Gatacre (known as 'Backacher' because of his gruelling physical expectations of his men) was sent to deal with the situation. What followed was an almost farcical demonstration of how not to fight a battle. Troops were left standing around for hours in the hot sun, other troops didn't get the message to turn up, Gatacre

Citizenship of the Transvaal meant that John Moody Lane, an Irishman, was obliged to fight for the Boers.

himself got hopelessly lost in the dark, and after a relatively bloodless retreat he realized that he had left more than 600 men up a mountain without telling them that he was going. Given their equally poor performance, the Boers were particularly fortunate to end up with a bag of 696 of Her Majesty's troops.

The next day it was to be the turn of Lord Methuen. After licking the wounds inflicted by the Boers at Modder River, he had now increased his force to 13,000 with a brigade of Highlanders under the popular commander Major-General Andrew Wauchope.

Methuen had been keeping a close eye on a small number of Boers who were evidently entrenching on the slopes of the 60-metre hill at Magersfontein. As Methuen set to work on a plan of attack, John Moody Lane could have given him some useful advice:

> There is a rumour in this morning it is the intention of the British to force their way thro' to Kimberley...If we are tackled by a flanking movement, it will be all up with the Boers. But a frontal attack will be fatal to the British, as the Boers are too well entrenched. It won't be so easy to make the wily Boer 'break cover'. In a trench with these Mausers they are devils to shoot, and having cartridges ad lib, he makes them fly.

The experience at Modder River had convinced De la Rey that trenches were the ideal way of wreaking havoc among the British. On the plains in front of Magersfontein he set to work building 20 kilometres of trench narrow and deep enough to provide his men with shelter from British shrapnel. Barbed wire entanglements were put into place and, as the finishing touch, bushes and branches were added to keep the Boers hidden from view.

As the Boers dug in, Methuen began his preparations. Bringing to bear all the artillery he could

Major-General Andrew Wauchope was killed as he commanded the Highland Brigade at Magersfontein.

muster, he directed a relentless daytime bombardment on the slopes of Magersfontein Hill. As the new high-explosive lyddite sent plumes of earth and rock fifteen metres up in the air, Methuen could only guess at the demoralization this show of force must be causing, and the number of casualties it must be inflicting.

In fact, the number of casualties was three, and all Methuen had succeeded in doing was to warn the Boers that an infantry attack was imminent. In the small hours of the next morning, 11 December, Wauchope led 4,000 men in close formation to spearhead the attack. The Black Watch, followed by the Seaforth Highlanders, followed by the Argylls and the Highland Light

Infantry made an impressive sight as ninety-six lines of green kilts made their way towards the foot of Magersfontein Hill.

It was 4 a.m. and Wauchope was just beginning to deploy his troops into attack formations when the air around them was suddenly torn apart by thousands of Mauser bullets. They seemed to be coming from beneath the Highlanders' very feet. As one sergeant put it, it was like 'someone had pressed a button and turned on a million electric lights'. Captain L. March Phillipps was there with Rimington's Guides:

> The fire came focused on a mass of men, such a fire as I suppose has never been seen before, for not only was it a tremendous volley poured in at point-blank range, but it was a sustained volley; the rapid action of the magazines enabling the enemy to keep up an intermittent hail of bullets on the English column. To advance under fire of this sort is altogether impossible. It is not a question of courage, but of the impossibility of a single man surviving…What the devil's the use of the bravest man with half-a-dozen bullets through him?

The firing was so rapid that it seemed like machine guns, but it was aimed too high, and many of the Highlanders who had not been hit fled back into the path of the Seaforths, spreading panic and resulting in a mass stampede to a line of bushes.

Wauchope, meanwhile, noticed a gap in the line of Boer fire and tried to send reinforcements through it. This was to be his last order before he himself was shot dead. About a hundred men actually managed to break through the line and started to climb the hill. For a moment it looked as though the Highlanders could reverse their fortunes, but then fate intervened. Cronje and no more than seven men had been wandering around on the hill and quite by chance came upon the British. Their Mauser-fire, combined with British artillery mistakenly firing on their own men, ensured that the only hope of escape from this nightmare was dashed.

About half the Highland Brigade remained on the plains, and as the sun rose higher in the sky, glinting on their canteen tins, they were fired on at point-blank range as they bravely attempted to take the Boers' trenches. Their attempts were futile, though, and for the rest of the morning they were pinned motionless to the ground. Michael Hefer's father Louis was in the Bloemfontein Artillery:

> My father told me that it was an incredibly hot day in the trenches…He said that their rifles got so hot that the Mauser had to be aimed already when the bullets got fed into the chamber because as soon as the bolt was closed the rifle would fire automatically.

The Seaforth Highlanders who had fled after the first

Kruger's intense gaze, in this German depiction, is melting the British 'tin soldier'.

Boer volley now rallied and, to the encouragement of the bagpipes, tried to take another part of the trench line.

John Moody Lane was in the Boer trenches:

> The slaughter, up to now, must be awful, still it never seems to cease, there they come on, again and again, against a hidden face. No man can call the British soldier a coward, seeing the way these men faced simply a hell, no turning back. I can see what must be the officers, urging their men on, springing in front, then I see hands thrown up, and fall, never to rise again. The other's taking the fallen one's place, to meet the same fate.

This was a new situation for the entrenched Boers. They had sacrificed all mobility and with it any possibility of a swift retreat – it was now kill or be killed. Rina Viljoen's father was in the artillery:

> **For him it was a very memorable battle. All the Boers were lying in trenches or behind big boulders. My**

The use of trenches by the Boers proved decisive in their victory at Magersfontein.

father was lying behind a rock and he told us how nerve-racking it was. The Scots with their drawn bayonets stormed against them. And they [the Boers] had orders that each one had to shoot his man, or else be stabbed to death by the Scots. And you could not shoot too soon. The distance had to be just right. And they had to wait for the command, because the Scots attacked in groups. And so the battle progressed. That day they killed many Scotsmen. My father told me how impressed he was by the bravery of the soldiers. He told us they were the bravest soldiers he encountered during the war.

Lord Methuen's advice to these brave soldiers was that 'they should hold on until nightfall'. A detachment of Gordons was ordered to charge through them at the trenches but, whatever morale boost this may have provided, the prostrate Highlanders cracked in the early afternoon as the

A STIFF LITTLE SHOW   63

Boers began an attack on their right. One officer described what happened:

> I saw a sight I hope I may never see again; men of the Highland Brigade running for all they were worth, others cowering under bushes, behind the guns, some lying under their blankets, officers running about with revolvers in their hands threatening to shoot them, urging on some, kicking on others; staff officers galloping about giving incoherent and impracticable orders.

As the afternoon wore on, the firing gradually died down until an armistice was agreed to collect the dead and wounded. Hundreds of men who had managed to escape the Boers' bullets were crippled for days afterwards because of the effects of the sun on the backs of their legs. Private Hall was one of the Gordon Highlanders trapped on the ground:

> We lay there all day in the scorching sun, and when the word was passed to retire we could hardly walk, as there were blisters hanging over our hose-tops.

Louis Hefer took no great pleasure in the Boers' success. He later wrote:

> I got up and walked over to where some of the Scottish troops were lying. Some of them had up to seven bullet holes through the head…For us Boers it was a very big victory, but it affected me deeply, very deeply when I looked around and saw all those young men scattered there.

L. March Phillipps also had time to reflect on what had happened:

> The Brigade was asked to do too much and when they at last staggered out of action, the men jumped and started at the rustle of a twig. It's a miserable thing when brave men are asked to do more than brave men can do.
> One thing that added to the panic was that none,

at least among the men and junior officers, knew anything at all about the trench. They thought they were going to storm the hill. So things were so contrived that the bewilderment of a surprise should be added to the terrors of a volley…We could scarcely have provided all the elements of a panic more carefully.

The British suffered nearly 1,000 casualties at Magersfontein, the Boers nearly 250. Lord Methuen was later to cause much bitterness among his men by hinting that the action could have been successful had it not been for the reaction of the Highlanders. The Highlanders felt equally let down by Methuen. A Black Watch private dictated a powerful poem from his hospital bed:

The Black Watch at Magersfontein
Such was the day for our regiment,
Dread the revenge we will take.
Dearly we paid for the blunder of a
Drawing-room general's mistake.

Where was the gallant general?
Three miles in rear out of sight.
No men to issue up orders,
Men doing what they thought right.

Why weren't we told of the trenches?
Why weren't we told of the wire?
Why were we marched up in column?
May Tommy Atkins enquire.

Do they know this in old England?
Do they know his incompetence yet?
Tommy has learned to his sorrow
And Tommy will never forget.

The Battle of Magersfontein stopped Lord Methuen's march to Kimberley in its tracks and he retreated back to the Modder River. The impatient

Cecil Rhodes at his diamond-mines was going to have to wait a little longer.

After two major disasters in the Cape, it was now up to the British Commander-in-Chief, Sir Redvers Buller, to force his way northwards through Natal and relieve Ladysmith. But General Botha was now at Colenso with 6,500 men. In order to get past them, Buller would need to cross the Tugela River, and take the town.

The force that Buller assembled was the biggest that had gone into battle for fifty years. With sixteen battalions, cavalry and heavy guns, Buller had 20,000 men at his disposal. The question was how best to use them. A Boer prisoner later said of the British:

> We could always tell what you were going to do. You would bombard our trenches for a time. Then your

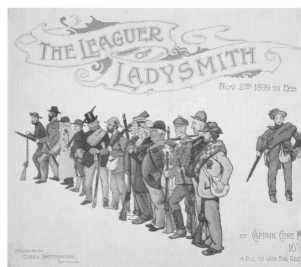

Captain Clive Dixon was besieged in Ladysmith when he sketched the illustrations for his book The Leaguer of Ladysmith *published in 1900.*

Opposite: The disastrous experience of the Highlanders at
Magersfontein was represented here by Richard
Caton Woodville.
Above: This watercolour depicts the attempt to save the guns
at Colenso which cost Lord Roberts' son, Freddy, his life.

soldiers would march straight at us. It was very brave
but *verdomd* foolish.

This time was to be no different.

Buller's plan was for a two-pronged attack. The Second Brigade under General Hildyard would take Colenso and the railway bridge, while the Fifth Brigade under Major-General Hart would take Bridle Drift on the left. The Fourth and the Sixth Brigades would act as general support from the rear.

The course of events was painfully similar to that at Modder River and Magersfontein – the Boers made use of the land and dug themselves in along the Tugela River. The British spent two days bombarding them, with no effect except to alert them to their intentions, before being ambushed with neither adequate maps nor intelligence. This time they did not walk into the ambush – they galloped into it. Colonel Long, who was in charge of the artillery, decided that the most effective way to mount the attack would be to push the guns right to the front of the infantry and blast the Boers with short-range fire. Leaving his escort far behind, he rode to within 650 metres of the river bank and was promptly ambushed by the entrenched Boers. The infantry had been left more than a kilometre behind, leaving Long and his twelve badly positioned field guns as the only targets. As their ammunition dwindled with no sign of the ammunition wagons, the men were forced to abandon their guns and to fall back to take cover.

Meanwhile, Major-General Hart and the Irish Brigade had set off towards Bridle Drift. Having no proper map, he relied on a native guide to show him to where he was going to cross the Tugela. Hart firmly believed in the virtues of keeping the men 'well in hand', so the brigade was in close formation as the guide mistakenly led it into the 'loop' of land that reached forward within range of the Boer positions. As more and more men packed in to within 180 metres of the river, the Boers started firing, literally from right, left and centre. Undeterred, Hart pressed his men to advance even further into the loop. It was only when Buller saw what was happening and ordered Hart to retire that the advance stopped. There had been 400 casualties in just forty minutes.

When Buller heard about the loss of the guns he decided to call the whole thing off and try to retrieve what amounted to half of his artillery. Without it there would be no hope of relieving Ladysmith anyway. Some brave volunteers attempted to ride across open country to rescue them, but they were soon wounded and beaten back. In broad daylight and with no attempt to disable Long's twelve field guns, Buller's entire army retired.

> **We were greatly disappointed to receive the following general order this evening. Sir Geo White regrets to inform the garrison of Ladysmith that Sir Redvers Buller failed to make good his first attack on Colenso (15th). He however hopes and trusts that Officers, Non-Commissioned Officers, and men of the garrison will carry on the defence of Ladysmith in the same spirited manner until its relief by the C in Chief in S. Africa.**

What Corporal James Cowland did not record in his diary for 17 December was that the 'C in Chief in S. Africa' had already contacted the War Office and Sir George White with his view that 'I ought

The Boers felt that the war to preserve their independence was blessed by God.

to let Ladysmith go'. Buller later argued that he did not mean that Ladysmith should be given up but that he should find a different approach. But the damage was done and the cable, on top of the disasters of Black Week, cost him his job. Buller was demoted to Commander in Natal. In his place was appointed Lord Roberts of Kandahar, whose son Freddy had been one of those killed while trying to rescue the guns at Colenso.

Morale at Ladysmith was badly dented. The guns of Colenso had been audibly close, and the novelty of the situation had by now worn off even for the *Daily Mail* correspondent, G. W. Steevens:

> At first, to be besieged and bombarded was a thrill; then it was a joke; now it is nothing but a weary, weary, weary bore. We do nothing but eat and drink and sleep – just exist dismally. We have forgotten when the siege began; and now we are beginning not to care when it ends. For my part I feel it will never end.

The day after Colenso was a special day for the Boers. 16 December was Dingaans' Day – the day on which the Battle of Blood River had been

fought in 1838. On all fronts burghers on commando took comfort from that victory against
such overwhelming odds. John Moody Lane's
commander was in bullish mood:

> After service was over, General with hat off gave the
> burghers an address of an hour's duration, going over
> the old, old story, how their forefathers had suffered at
> the hands of the 'rooinek', how they had shed their
> blood for 'freedom' and 'right', and winding up with
> thank God the time had now come, when the
> 'rooinek' must be driven into the sea, and he would do
> it, and be in Cape Town in a month's time, where the
> 'rooinek' must come begging on his knees for peace.

'Rooinek' was how the Boers referred to the
British, whose necks would turn red and burn
under the South African sun.

Fransjohan Pretorius is an expert on the
Afrikaner aspects of the war. Both his grandfathers
were on commando:

> It was quite clear that the Boers felt satisfied with the
> 'Black Week' victories. And although they celebrated
> these victories with gratitude, it was the phlegmatic
> even temper of the Boer that was evident. The foreign
> members of the volunteer corps were astounded that
> the Boers were not elated about these victories. But it
> was just part of God's plan. It is as it should be. We
> were good shots with the help of God. This slogan,
> 'With the help of God', almost became a life's
> philosophy.

Ada Prinsloo, whose father was on commando,
confirms that prayer was used almost as a tactic:

> When the commander was praying before they got on
> to the battlefield, they would ask Jesus to protect every
> burgher. And that He must please give them the
> power to fight against a superior power and that we
> please want to hold on to our country…The Boers

were in a small minority but lived very close to Jesus
…During every battle they believed that Jesus was
fighting alongside them and I think quite often that
was the case because a couple of Boers would often
fight against huge numbers and after some time the
English [sic] would raise the white flag and surrender.

Back in Britain the public were shocked at the
bloody nose given to 'the soldiers of the Queen'.
The largest British expeditionary force in history
had thus far come off second best to a primitive
bunch of farmers from two of the smallest countries in the world. Because of the recent advances
in telegraphy, every blunder and reverse could be
written up overnight and disseminated to the
news-hungry public by the next morning. But
almost as demoralizing as the bad news itself was
the gloating of Britain's European rivals. The wave
of virulent anti-British sentiment in the German
and French press prompted the Birmingham
Daily Mail to declare:

> Stalwart Englishmen armed with good horsewhips
> should go to France and administer a severe castiga-
> tion to the vulgar crowds…The Parisian, like a dog,
> barks loudest in his own kennel.

Black Week did have one positive effect in Britain
– it made the task of recruitment much easier. The
War Office was still in a shambles, and equipping
the first army corps had pushed it to its limit.
Now, as commander in Natal, Buller was demanding 8,000 mounted men, and there were plans to
send out another 45,000 reinforcements. As a
wave of patriotism swept the country, the problem
of procuring more mounted men was solved by
the establishment of the Imperial Yeomanry. The
new volunteers came predominantly from the
middle classes, giving rise to small companies of
men like Lord Lathom's Roughriders, Earl
Dunraven's Battalion of Sharpshooters and the

Duke of Cambridge's Own who paid for their passage to South Africa and donated their wages to the Widows and Orphans Fund. The infantry and artillery were also reinforced with volunteers, the most famous group being the City Imperial Volunteers.

But it was not just Britain that rallied to the call. Millions of pounds and thousands of men came from Canada, Australia and New Zealand. This was the first time that the Empire, or at least the white parts of it, had gone to war. 'Foreign' help was not restricted to the British side. Many Europeans, particularly from Holland and Germany, but also Scandinavia, France and Russia, went to show solidarity with the Boers in the struggle between Republican David and Imperialist Goliath. There were even Irish republicans. They were often a little surprised by their reception as the Boers' insularity had not diminished with the outbreak of war. President Kruger's welcome to a group of volunteers from Germany was not untypically graceless:

Thank you for coming. Don't imagine that we had need of you. Transvaal wants no foreign help, but as you wish to fight for us you are welcome. I take your coming as a gratifying sign that Europe is gradually beginning to recognize the right of the Afrikaner nation.

So as Christmas came and went and the sieges continued in Mafeking, Kimberley and Ladysmith. One shell fired into Ladysmith by the Boers even contained, on closer inspection, a plum pudding wrapped in a Union Jack.

Despite the Boer successes of Black Week, not everything in the Cape had gone as they had

After receiving the news about Black Week Queen Victoria remarked, 'We are not interested in the possibilities of defeat.'

Overleaf: Crossing and recrossing the Tugela River would earn Buller the nickname 'The Ferryman of the Tugela'.

planned. The 40,000 Cape rebels who had been expected to rise up numbered only 7,000. As more and more British reinforcements arrived, it was clear to the Boers that they were short of men, especially with so many tied up around the siege towns. In January, the decision was taken to storm Ladysmith, thus freeing up some of the besieging commandos. Success depended on the Boers taking the hills around the town, but the operation ultimately failed because, of the 4,000 men ordered by Botha to storm Wagon Hill, only a few hundred obeyed. According to Fransjohan Pretorius:

One of the most outstanding characteristics of commando life, in retrospect, was the absence of discipline. The Boer is a strong individualist – 'Every Boer is his own general.' And it often happened that an officer would say: 'Take that hill!' He would be talking to a commando of 150 men. Then 50 men would go and take the hill. The other 100 would go home, put their feet up, make coffee, cook a meal, saying, 'We'll catch up with you later.'

Although the Boers failed to take Ladysmith, it was a close-run thing and it prompted Sir George White to inform Buller that he would not be able to commit any of his forces to a relief effort as they were too depleted.

Buller had been on the defensive since Colenso, but it was now apparent that unless he had another go at relieving White at Ladysmith, the Boers' next attempt at storming the town might well be successful. By mid-January 1900 30,000 men had been amassed for another attempt to break through the Tugela line.

From the heights of Mount Alice on the south side of the Tugela River, Sir Redvers Buller could look ahead and see Ladysmith, only 30

kilometres away. Between him and the open plains that led to the town lay two major obstacles: the river itself and the range of mountains known as the Drakensberg. The best way through involved crossing the river at Trichardt's Drift, then taking the road that led between two vast peaks to the plains beyond.

To the left stood the high hill called Tabanyama and to the right was the highest peak in the Drakensberg range – Spion Kop. It was from the 460-metre summit of Spion Kop, or 'Scouts Hill', that the Voortrekkers had first looked down on the rolling plains of Natal.

Buller decided to split his army into two. The largest force, to be led by Sir Charles Warren, would go over Trichardt's Drift and follow the road round behind Spion Kop. The lesser force, under Buller, would wait until Warren was clear of the hills and then cross the river further east at Potgieter's Drift, where they would join forces and

proceed to Ladysmith. It is still not clear why Buller effectively placed the success or failure of the operation in Warren's hands. He did not admire his qualities as a general and did not even particularly like him. Whatever the reason, it was a decision that Buller would live to regret.

The key to the success of this operation would be the speed at which Warren crossed the Tugela, as it was the perfect opportunity to take advantage of the relatively low number of Boers in the area.

On 16 January Warren set out for Trichardt's Drift. Despite being unmolested by the Boers, Warren did not seem to be in any particular hurry and it took him two days to construct and put in place the bridges that would get his men across the Tugela. On reaching the other side, he then spent another two days trying to decide whether to go round Tabanyama or whether to make a frontal assault. An invaluable opportunity was missed when Lord Dundonald and his mounted troops

Above: *The Boers outside Ladysmith successfully kept up the pressure on Sir George White.*
Right: *Lieutenant-Colonel Andrew Thorneycroft led the initial British ascent of Spion Kop.*

reconnoitred the left side of Tabanyama and discovered no Boers in sight. He immediately sent to Warren for reinforcements to take the hill, but Warren refused – it was not the job of mounted troops to talk about taking hills – and he called them back and tore a strip off Dundonald for exceeding his brief. Instead, Warren decided to try a frontal assault. By this time, of course, Louis Botha had been alerted to the unwieldy British presence and had sent reinforcements. Warren had needlessly lost his element of surprise and then lost 470 of his men in an abortive effort to take Tabanyama from the now well-entrenched Boers.

It was now 22 January and Warren had made no progress at all. Buller, who had been drumming his fingers impatiently at Mount Alice, rode forward to tell Warren to get a move on. Warren suggested that he take Spion Kop instead of Tabanyama; Buller agreed in the interests of getting things moving. This was a critical decision that intelligent scouting would have shown to be the wrong one. Although Spion Kop was only a little higher than the surrounding peaks, it was so steep that it was impossible to drag any heavy guns to the top. If only the reconnaissance balloon had been sent up to give some indication of the scale of the task facing them, Warren and Buller would surely have avoided the bloodiest episode of the war.

At 11 p.m. on the night of 23 January about 1,900 men under General Sir Edward Woodgate began the ascent of Spion Kop. They were led by Lieutenant-Colonel Alexander Thorneycroft and his corps of Uitlander mounted infantry who, on this tricky climb, were forced to leave their horses behind. Absolute stealth was essential if the men were to reach the summit without alerting the Boers. Matthew Kelly of the South Lancashire Regiment recorded the climb in his diary:

Not a word is allowed to be spoken. All the dogs which are following us are destroyed. After marching

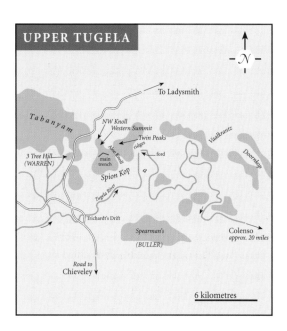

The relief of Ladysmith required the British forces to cross the Tugela River and negotiate a passage through the hills of Tabanyama and Spion Kop.

for two or three hours we are told quietly that we have passed the enemies' sentries and are in their lines...It is very steep, so steep in fact that our ammunition mules fall backwards in attempting to climb it.

After dispensing with a Boer picket on the way, Woodgate and his men had managed to reach the summit with apparent ease. The prearranged signal of three cheers was given to inform Warren of their success. In the dark and the mist, a trench was taped out and the men began to dig. Unfortunately, many of the tools had been abandoned on the way up because they were too heavy, and the twenty spades that were left soon hit a bed of igneous rock only a matter of centimetres beneath the surface. To make matters worse, the sandbags that were supposed to have been brought up with the men had been left at the bottom.

Meanwhile, the surviving members of the Boer

picket had raced back down Spion Kop to tell Botha and the other Boer commander, Schalk Burger, that the summit was swarming with Khakis. Burghers were pulled back from Ladysmith, big guns were placed on the surrounding heights and the decision was taken to retake the hill at all costs.

After the abortive attempt to dig a deep trench, the British on Spion Kop snatched a couple of hours' rest before dawn broke. The *Manchester Guardian* correspondent described them as being on a 'fog-bound island in the air'. Then, just after 7 a.m., there was a break in the mist and Woodgate realized that they had taken only part of the summit. But it was not until the mist lifted an hour later that Woodgate and his men, including Matthew Kelly, were made aware of just how severe his error had been:

> About 8 a.m. the Boers open a terrific fire...from every place except our extreme rear. We take the best cover we can get. Capt. Birch of my company gets shot in the head just above the eye. The fire is terrible; ever so much heavier than what I had seen before or since.

The main trench, which was no more that a shallow depression, was in completely the wrong place, about 180 metres from the summit edge. Not only did the Boers have the ground around it, but they proceeded to rake the summit with fire from the surrounding heights of Green Hill, Twin Peaks and Aloe Knoll.

Despite having ten times more artillery than the Boers, the British had no big guns on Spion Kop and found it almost impossible to hit the Boers' Pom-Poms and Long Tom, which were doing so much damage.

But in the face of this constant bombardment, the British at the top fought a bloody battle with the Boers, who streamed up to the summit under the cover of the precipitous slopes of Spion Kop.

Seventeen-year-old Deneys Reitz, whose vivid account of the war was later published, was in the Pretoria commando sent to try to retake the crest. On his way up he passed his friends from the commando, who had been killed making the ascent. After taking the crest, Reitz was forced to dig in at almost point-blank range:

> The moral effect of Lee-Metford volleys at twenty yards must be experienced to be appreciated. The

Seventeen-year-old Deneys Reitz wrote a vivid account of his experiences during the war.

English troops lay so near that one could have tossed a biscuit among them, and whilst the losses which they were causing us were only too evident, we on our side did not know that we were inflicting even greater damage upon them, but theirs were screened from view behind the breastwork, so that the comfort of knowing that we were giving worse than we received was denied us.

At 8.45 a.m. General Woodgate was felled by a piece of shrapnel to the head. He had just sent a message to Warren requesting water and reinforcements, but because of the slowness of the signallers Warren did not receive the message for another hour. After a number of officers were lost, the command of the hill fell to the senior man, Colonel Crofton. His first act was to tell another signaller to ask for help. The message Warren received read:

Colonel Crofton to G.O.C. Force. Reinforce at once or all lost. General dead.

Luckily, Warren, on hearing the noise from the summit, had already sent up reinforcements under Major-General Talbot Coke before Crofton's message arrived. But the tone of the message concerned him. It sounded as though Crofton had lost his head. Warren and Buller decided to replace him with Thorneycroft. A signal was sent informing Crofton, but no one thought to tell Talbot Coke who then had no idea who was in charge. This lack of effective communication was to be a theme running through the British experience at Spion Kop. It was clear that Warren had absolutely no idea of the seriousness of the situation on the summit. He could not see it from his camp. At one point he even stopped an effective barrage from the naval guns because he thought they were firing on their own men. He simply did not know that the Boers had possession of so much of the ridge.

Meanwhile, at the summit Botha's guns were dropping shells on the British at a rate of ten per minute. Private Thomas Cook wrote:

This was the fatal Spion Kop & [with] the sun pouring down today, this was a sight to see – the shells dropping everywhere. You could see the poor chaps shot down like skittle pins falling down... 2 of our companies had to go up to dig trenches but soon had to come down again. This is one of the worst days that I have ever seen but expect to have some more before this is over.

By the middle of the day, with the sun beating down, no sign of water and the relentless pounding of the shells, a few British soldiers at the end of the line began to raise white flags and offer themselves as prisoners. Catching sight of what was going on, the limping figure of Thorneycroft hobbled down the line, yelling: 'Take your men back to hell, sir! There's no surrender.'

It was just in the nick of time, then, that the reinforcements arrived. Captain Colin Pritchard had been seconded to the Imperial Light Infantry. He proudly wrote home:

I know that I was the first man of the reinforcements...I had a zipping lot of men with me, among them my friend Hastings. When I had once selected a place for my men I didn't lose a single man – killed or wounded. The Company behind me, not 80 yards away, lost 17 killed! The Boers got a 'pom pom' or Vickers Maxim to play upon them and the sights we saw were ghastly.

In the breathing space afforded by the arrival of the reinforcements, Thorneycroft was able to send a dispatch to Warren:

...can you not bring artillery to bear on NW guns? What reinforcements can you send me to hold the hill

The British and Boers came together after the battle to tend to the wounded on both sides.

tonight, we are badly in need of water, there are many killed and wounded. If you really wish to make certainty of hill for the night you must send more infantry and attack enemy guns.

But the respite did not last for long, and the Boers soon renewed their offensive with even more vigour. Having swept the British from the right of the summit, they then began to bear down on the main British trench from behind. Once again reinforcements prevented a mass surrender. Talbot Coke, recovering from a broken leg, was still making his way to the top when he read Thorneycroft's dispatch as it came down.

By 4.30 in the afternoon, both sides were exhausted, and both sides believed themselves to be losing.

We were hungry, thirsty and tired; around us were the dead men covered with swarms of flies attracted by the smell of blood. We did not know the cruel losses that the English were suffering, and we believed that they were easily holding their own, so discouragement spread as the shadows lengthened.

Deneys Reitz's description of how the Boers were feeling applied equally to the British. Winston Churchill, as well as fulfilling his correspondent's duties, had also joined the South African Light Horse. He rode over to Spion Kop to see what was happening and was shocked by what he found:

Men were staggering along alone, or supported by comrades, or crawling on hands and knees, or carried on stretchers. Corpses lay here and there...The splinters and fragments of shell had torn and mutilated in the most ghastly manner. I passed about two hundred while I was climbing up. There was, moreover, a small but steady leakage of unwounded men of all corps. Some of these cursed and swore. Others were utterly exhausted and fell on the hillside in stupor. Others again seemed drunk, though they had had no liquor.

This leakage became even greater among the Boers when the King's Royal Rifles managed to pull off a diversionary tactic that gave them control of the adjoining Twin Peaks. This operation was the only time any attempt was made by the British to take the heat away from the battle on the summit and, in fact, was carried out only because the commanding officer turned a deaf ear to the orders telling him to come back.

If communication had been better and Thorneycroft had been kept informed of what was going on, the outcome might have been very different. As it was, he did not receive one direct communication from Warren for the entire duration of the battle and consequently was left demoralized and unsure of what to do. At 6.00 p.m. he sent another dispatch to Warren:

The troops which marched uphill last night are quite done up...they have no water, ammunition is running short. I consider that even with reinforcements which have arrived it is impossible to permanently hold this place so long as the enemy's guns play on the hill.

As night fell, both sides were faced with the consequences of the havoc they had wreaked on one another. Thorneycroft had still not received any stretcher-bearers and so Captain Pritchard, who had gone up with the reinforce-

ments of the Imperial Light Infantry, was among those moving the dead and injured:

After 8 o'clock when the firing ceased and we could rest a little, the cries of the wounded were ghastly. That's where the horrors of war come in and they have to be seen to be understood...we put the body down between two others we found – one headless and the other minus both legs! But after the squeaks that you had had yourself during the day, such sights had no effect on you – at least I, who can't take ugly sights in cold blood, never even squirmed except when I crawled through the remains of that disembowelled man.

Churchill, who had gone straight from Spion Kop to alert Warren to Thorneycroft's plight, volunteered to go back up to the top with a reassuring note promising big guns, ammunition, water and 1,400 men. He got there to find Thorneycroft intent on coming down. After twelve hours of bloody, ceaseless killing, the British retired from Spion Kop. Even

On the other side of Spion Kop, the Boers were unaware that the British were deserting the ridge at the same time as they were.

when they met the reinforcements who had been sent up to join them, they could not be stopped. On being shown a note from Warren urging him to hold on at all costs, Thorneycroft simply said: 'I have done all I can and I am not going back.'

The dreadful irony was that exactly the same scene was being played out on the other side of the hill. Convinced of their defeat, Boers were streaming down the slopes of Spion Kop until the indefatigable Louis Botha rode from laager to laager exhorting his men to reoccupy their positions. It worked. But as a small group of Boers, including Deneys Reitz, started the ascent, they were met with an amazing sight:

Gradually the dawn came...to our utter surprise we

Above and opposite: The British lost almost 2,000 men at Spion Kop, and the Boers almost 200.

saw two men on the top triumphantly waving their hats and holding their rifles aloft. They were Boers, and their presence there was proof that, almost unbelievably, defeat had turned to victory – the English were gone and the hill was still ours.

The Boers had taken the hill through a stroke of luck. If the British had happened to wander back up Spion Kop to find its only inhabitants the dead of the day before, then the hill would have been theirs instead.

The day's fighting had cost the British between 1,800 and 2,000 men either dead, wounded or

captured. The Boers had lost 198. As the stretcher-bearers and burial parties set about their grim tasks, Deneys Reitz surveyed the scene on the summit of Spion Kop:

> The soldiers lay dead in swathes, and in places they were piled three deep. The Boer guns in particular had wrought terrible havoc and some of the bodies were shockingly mutilated. There must have been six hundred dead men on this strip of earth, and there cannot have been many battlefields where there was such an accumulation of horrors within so small a compass.

The wounded were taken by Indian stretcher bearers including Mohandas Gandhi to the field hospital, recognizable by two lamps suspended from flagpoles. One of the surgeons there was Frederick Treves, surgeon to the Queen. He described the aftermath of Spion Kop in his book *Diary of a Field Hospital*:

> Some were asleep and some were dead; and by the light of the lanterns the waggon seemed full of khaki-coloured bundles, vague of outline, and much stained with blood, with here and there an upraised bandage, and here and there a wandering hand, or a leg in crude splints, or a bare knee... A man with a shattered arm in a sling was sitting up, and at his feet a comrade was lying who had been very hard hit, and who had evidently become weaker and less conscious as the waggon had rolled along. This apparently sleeping man moved, and, lifting his head to look at his pal...

LITERACY

BRITAIN'S LAST MAJOR CONFLICT had been the Crimean War of 1854. Since then there had been significant social change. The Education Act of 1870 provided a framework for compulsory elementary education, and its effects were far-reaching. The literacy rate shot up from 63.3 per cent in 1841 to 92.2 per cent in 1900. As Britain went to war in 1899 this new literacy would alter the way in which wars were reported. As one author wrote:

> Never before has Britain sent forth to the battlefield so large a force of men sufficiently educated to write home. The war therefore has been described from day to day, not like all other wars, by professional journalists or by literary officers but by the rank and file.

The new outpouring of writing was met with an equal appetite for reading it. This was the time when modern popular journalism came into its own. The *Daily Mail* had been launched in 1896 promising to 'explain, simplify, clarify'. Within just three years it had double the circulation of any other national newspaper, and its commitment to the 'supremacy and greatness of the British Empire' combined with its affordability ('a penny newspaper for one halfpenny') meant that the *Mail* could not have arrived at a better time. Nothing increases circulation like a good war: in

Below: *A new standard of literacy in Britain meant that the rank and file in the British Army could record their day-to-day experiences as never before.*
Opposite: *A thirst for news and the birth of the popular press meant that newspaper correspondents were always in demand in South Africa.*

1898 430,000 people were buying the *Mail* every day; by 1900 it was almost a million.

Arthur Whitlock, a small boy at the time, remembers taking advantage of one of the gimmicks designed to pull in more readers:

> I was able to follow the war more closely because the *Daily Mail*, they brought out a map, and you had little flags with pins on them, so you could pin these coloured flags…and you pinned them showing the position of the various troops. We would move those pins and those flags about on this map in the same way as you saw them in the later wars in the control rooms, moving their various positions, with a pointer and suchlike. And I did more or less the same thing with my miniature map on the table.

Satisfying the needs of the new British readership was not confined to the *Daily Mail*. Fifty-eight newspaper correspondents accompanied the main British army to South Africa; *The Times* alone had twenty correspondents there. One young journalist had even managed to get a letter of recommendation sent by Joseph Chamberlain to Sir Alfred Milner:

> I am sending a line to anticipate a probable visit from Winston Churchill, the son of Lord Randolph Churchill, who is going out as a correspondent for the *Morning Post*…He is a very clever young fellow with many of his father's qualifications. He has the reputation of being bumptious, but I have myself not found him so, and time will no doubt get rid of the defect if he has it…He is a good writer and full of energy. He hopes to be in Parliament, but want of means stand in the way.

asked wearily, for probably the fiftieth time, 'Don't you see nothing yet, Bill, of the two white lights?'

As the wounded were treated, and the dead were buried, Boers sang psalms and said prayers for those who had died on both sides. But further down the hill the Boer heliographer Louis Bothma was being given instructions by Commandant Hendryk Prinsloo. The heliograph was a simple signalling device mounted on a tripod that used the sun's rays and a mirror to flash morse code over a distance.

> When the sun rose he again ordered me to flash my signals to headquarters. I had to flash my signals across Ladysmith, and a signaller from the town answered. I quickly made it clear to him that they could not count on deliverance by Gen. Buller, as we stood between them and 1,500 of their dead.

Above: Mohandas Gandhi managed to raise an ambulance force of 1,100 Indian volunteers.
Opposite: Soldiers also helped to carry the wounded.

Trapped in Ladysmith with all hopes of relief dashed once again, a captain in the rifle brigade wondered 'How on earth men who call themselves Englishmen [sic] could allow themselves to be turned off a hill by a pack of Dutch peasants'.

The Boers were not inclined to chase the British as they made their ignominious retreat back the way they came. Deneys Reitz stood and watched:

> Long columns of troops and long convoys of transport were re-crossing to the south bank, and everywhere the British were in full retreat from the positions which they had captured on this side of the stream, and the clouds of dust rising on the Colenso road told

us that General Buller's second great attempt to pierce the Tugela defences had failed.

The Lancashire regiments took such heavy losses in the battle that in 1906 a terrace at Liverpool football ground was christened Spion Kop in honour of the men who died there and has been known as 'The Kop' ever since. The Battle of Spion Kop itself stands as a monument to the faults of the British army in 1900. The bravery of the soldiers is unquestionable, but that bravery was often thrown away by generals who failed to carry out the most basic level of reconnaissance. They were even reduced to borrowing maps from the local school. Men were sent up Spion Kop without any idea of what they would find when they reached the top. They were left without any heavy artillery because of the impossibility of dragging it up the steep slopes, and the levels of communication were so poor that even the commanding officers did not know what was going on. At one point no fewer than three officers believed that they were in charge of the summit. Poor intelligence, lack of effective communication and poor generalship were as decisive as the Boer enemy in defeating the British that day.

The achievements of the Boers since the start of the war had been greater than anyone had expected. John Moody Lane was left to wonder:

Who are these people who defy such a mighty power as the British Empire: no military appearance; no discipline; some of them mere youths of twelve years of age, others old men…this crowd of all sorts and conditions have actually declared war and are now fighting the mighty nation of the world, and more than that, have actually got the winning points in their favour. Surely this will change.

Cecil Rhodes became increasingly troublesome to the British military during the siege of Kimberley.

CHAPTER FOUR

Turning the Tide

This was sport with a vengeance, better than seeing Aston Villa's left forward scoring the winning goal, or W.G. hitting three successive boundaries from the best Australian bowling.

J. B. LLOYD, AN INNS OF COURT VOLUNTEER

THE NEW COMMANDER-IN-CHIEF, Lord Roberts of Kandahar, and his Chief of Staff, Lord Kitchener of Khartoum, or Bobs and K as they were familiarly known, had landed at Cape Town on 10 January 1900. Roberts was already a national hero from his Indian exploits; even his horse had been awarded an Afghan War Medal by special direction of Queen Victoria. Kitchener was still glowing from his ruthlessly effective suppression of the dervishes at Omdurman. Bobs and K were both fully aware that Britain was expecting them to wipe away the memories of Black Week with a decisive victory over what the author Arthur Conan Doyle described as these 'hard-bitten farmers with their ancient theology and their inconveniently modern rifles'.

As every battle seemed to expose yet more weaknesses in the British army, even ordinary soldiers like Alec Kearsey could see ways in which matters could be improved:

It seems to me that the Boers have a pull over us in their administration as each commando gets his orders from the chief & has to act accordingly but with us there is a long chain of responsibility & before a move can be made all links have to be set going and in that way orders sometimes miscarry & if one of the links is knocked out - as Gen Woodgate on Spion Kop - in that

The arrival of Lord Roberts of Kandahar would mark a change in British fortunes.

unlucky retirement -- there is no one to take his place as no one knows what the Commander in Chief has ordered and wants done.

By early February Roberts had formulated his grand plan and had implemented the changes necessary to carry it out. He would move his force up the western railway line, relieve Kimberley and then swing east to Bloemfontein before advancing on Pretoria. With close to 180,000 men under his command, more than the entire Boer population, Roberts' strategy required comprehensive maps, accurate military intelligence and a reliable communication system. General French was given a new cavalry division, and the infantry were given lessons in basic horsemanship in an attempt to get as many of them mounted as possible. Roberts even issued a reminder of the lessons that had been learned so far during the war and laid emphasis on mobility, marksmanship and individual initiative.

It was a lack of exactly this individual initiative that doomed Buller's third attempt at crossing the Tugela River to failure. Ten days after Spion Kop and the withdrawal back across the river, the man who was being referred to as 'Sir Reverse Buller'

The basic requirements of horsemanship sometimes took a little time for the British to master.

and 'The Ferryman of the Tugela' decided to have another go at reaching Ladysmith. This time he would cross the Tugela River by pontoon bridge and head for a gap in the Drakensberg range at Vaalkrantz. Despite the fact that his forces numbered 20,000, compared with just over 1,500 Boers, Buller's continual hesitation and reluctance to press home his initial advantage resulted in Boers flooding in and Buller pulling out yet again.

Leaving Buller to hold his own in Natal, Roberts began his long march north on 11 February. For Captain L. March Phillipps of Rimington's Guides, the anticipation was finally over:

At last! Is everyone's feelings. The long waited for moment has come. You know a hawk's hover? Body steady, wings beating, and then the rushing swoop. So with the army. We have hovered steady here these two months with our wings stretched. Now we swoop.

In Kimberley, the news that Bobs was on his way came none too soon for Cecil Rhodes. Just two days earlier the commanding officer, Robert Kekewich, had been forced to send a telegram to Lord Roberts warning him that Rhodes was threatening to surrender the town. Roberts' response was to authorize Kekewich to arrest anyone, 'no matter what may be his position', who threatened the national interest.

But not only was Kekewich battling against Rhodes' high-handed attitude, he was also faced with the continuing, demoralizing bombardment of the town. Even one of the besiegers, John Moody Lane, had some sympathy for the inhabitants:

Report from Kimberley Laager: our big 100-pounder sent sixteen shells into the town this afternoon. There must have been a big fire there, as I could see the flames and smoke, some store I suppose on fire. Am sorry for the poor women and children.

Sanctuary from the Long Toms was provided courtesy of De Beers Consolidated Mines Ltd when Rhodes opened two of his mines to provide shelter for women and children. It was a magnanimous gesture, but if he had only told Kekewich of his plan he could also have equipped the mines with proper sanitation. Janice Farquharson's mother was one of those who sheltered there:

> My mother remembered that it seemed to be raining all the time. Now I think that was because the water table was very high and you got water coming down the shafts and the tunnel walls. And she also said that the loos were absolutely ghastly, and her mother used to have to piggyback each child in turn to the loos... that must have been one of the horrors of the siege.

Cecil Rhodes' generosity did not extend to the mine-workers, who were still languishing under wire netting in the Kimberley compounds. The war had made them redundant, but even if they had been able to afford food, the siege regulations prohibited them and all other Africans from buying meat or vegetables. The result was 1,500 cases of scurvy, one-third of which were fatal. Rhodes did organize soup kitchens, but in his opinion, with the whites reduced to eating horseflesh, there was still not enough food to go around. According to Janice Farquharson:

> There was no doubt that there was a difference between the rations given to the blacks and the rations given to the whites. The Boer women were actually offered open free passage out of Kimberley. And also Rhodes and Kekewich tried to encourage the blacks to leave. There is of course the classic story that some of the Boer generals said: 'No, you don't get out, you go back into Kimberley and you eat the food there.' In other words using the food there as a weapon.

This weapon would prove to be most deadly against small children. Kimberley's infant mortality rate showed that from October 1899 to mid-February 1900, fifty per cent of white babies and 93.5 per cent of black babies died.

As Roberts proceeded north, General Cronje was lying in wait for him at Magersfontein the scene of his victory two months before. Convinced of the British inability to move away from the railway line, he thought that Roberts must have been bluffing when the cavalry division suddenly swung out to the east and appeared on his left flank. But as a body of infantry and artillery also moved out to cover them, Cronje realized his mistake. It was too late, though, and in a cloud of dust and a hail of bullets 5,000 of French's finest cavalrymen galloped straight through the middle of the Boer lines towards Kimberley. On 15 February an advance party led by Major-General Broadwood, with the threat of Roberts' army behind him, dissolved the Boer presence around Kimberley, and the town was relieved.

As Roberts waited for news of French, he received a message that almost convinced him to completely abandon the march to Bloemfontein. One of Roberts' and Kitchener's less successful overhauls of the army had been to change the transport system from a localized one, in which each battalion was responsible for transporting its provisions, to a centralized one, in which an unwieldy train of oxen would pull the provisions for the whole column. After the gruelling effort of crossing the Riet River, the oxen were resting at Waterval Drift when the Boer commander, Christiaan de Wet – who would take an almost legendary status as the war progressed – appeared from nowhere and after a brief skirmish succeeded in stampeding most of the 3,000 oxen. The telegraph said that unless more men were sent back, Roberts would also lose the 170 wagons packed with food, medicine and other provisions vital to

Many burghers travelled in wagon trains or laagers with their wives, children and household goods.

the march. Roberts almost retreated back to the railway line there and then, but after taking advice and deciding that his men could get by on half-rations he pressed onwards.

Cronje, meanwhile, having failed to block Roberts at Magersfontein, decided to move his entire laager of 5,000 men, their families and 400 wagons to the east to try to stop the British march to Bloemfontein. Despite the fact that French's dash had practically wiped out the cavalry as a fighting force, the 1,200 horses that were not completely exhausted managed to make the 50-kilometre ride from Kimberley and intercept Cronje as his convoy made its painstaking way across the Modder River at Paardeberg.

Roberts, delayed by influenza, authorized Kitchener to take charge. General Kelly-Kenny, in charge of the Sixth Division, was keen to surround Cronje and bombard him into surrender, but Kitchener overruled him and ordered an all-out

direct offensive at the 8 kilometres of river Cronje was occupying. Early in the morning of 18 February came major attacks from the south and west, but the cover provided by the river bed resulted in two hours of bitter fighting and a failed advance. Then Kitchener ordered an attack from the east, which also resulted in much loss of life but no progress. The strategy was not working, and Kitchener was losing control. Having failed to make adequate preparations, he was unable to communicate his orders, and the battlefield fragmented into unrelated units. Despite a message from Colonel Hannay's exhausted Mounted Infantry saying that further advances were out of the question, Kitchener replied that the laager should be rushed at all costs. In the face of this response, Hannay kept his men at a distance and symbolically rode at full gallop into the Boer fire to be mown down as he knew his men would have been. Even this desperate act did not stop Kitchener from squandering more of his men's lives. At about 5 p.m., although it hardly seemed possible, the battle took a turn for the worse. Christiaan de Wet appeared and, by storming the hill known as Kitchener's Kopje, gained an important vantage point opposite the laager. The arrival of De Wet and another contingent of Boers gave Cronje renewed strength and the battle continued until nightfall.

In the first battle he had fought against white men, Kitchener had sustained almost 1,300 casualties with very little to show for them. The eighteenth of February saw the highest British casualty rate of the war, and Kitchener's profligate approach to the lives of his men, which would once again be demonstrated fourteen years later in his capacity as War Minister during the Great War.

Roberts arrived the next day and, following some initial hesitation, Kitchener's plans to renew the frontal assault were shelved. Instead, Cronje was encircled and bombarded while a concerted attempt was made to dislodge De Wet from Kitchener's Kopje.

Although Cronje's entrenchment in the river bank had kept casualty figures to a minimum, the morale in the Boer laager was low. Cronje's request for a truce in which the dead could be buried had been denied by Roberts, and the deafening bombardment by lyddite shells was relentless. The resolve of the besieged laager prompted Captain L. March Phillipps to write:

> Never tell me these Boers aren't brave. What manner of life, think you, is in yonder ditch? Our artillery rains down its crossfire of shells perpetually. The great ox-wagons are almost totally destroyed or burnt. The ammunition in the carts keeps blowing up as the fire reaches it. The beasts, horses and oxen, are strewn about, dead and putrid, and deserters say that the stench from their rotting carcasses is unbearable. Night and day they have to be prepared for infantry attacks, and yet, to the amazement of all of us, they still hold out.

Christiaan de Wet, high up on Kitchener's Kopje, was doing all he could to persuade Cronje to break out. But as the British began to encircle him, De Wet beat a hasty retreat to the nearby Poplar Grove. Rina Viljoen's father was a burgher fighting alongside De Wet:

> My father told us that they had sent a message to Cronje telling him that they were going to attack the English so that a safe passageway could be created. And as soon as they created that passageway, Cronje, with his commando, must flee. He should not take any wagons along, only his troops on horseback and as quick as possible. But Cronje never reacted. When that safe passage was created he just stayed put.

With 30,000 men surrounding him and conditions worsening every day, Cronje

This was the first war Lord Kitchener of Kandahar had fought against white men.

was having to direct all his energies to simply preventing his men from surrendering. John Moody Lane had reached the limits of his endurance:

> It is simply a hell here now, the stench is awful, we will be all down with fever, the river is full of dead horses, oxen, mules, as well as human corpses.

But against all the odds the laager refused to give in to the British, believing that each extra day they held out would enable more reinforcements to come and relieve them. L. March Phillipps knew that the Boers could never beat such overwhelming odds:

> The shells burst over them. The lyddite blows them up in smoke and dust, the sun grills, the dead bodies reek, our infantry creep up on them day and night; foul food; putrid water, death above and around, they

grin and bear it day after day to gain the precious hours. And all the time we on our side know perfectly well that no relief they could possibly bring up would serve our army for rations for a day.

It was the introduction of the Howitzers, with their 120-pound shells, that finally broke Cronje's resolve. At 6 a.m. on 27 February, John Moody Lane, with some sense of relief, took part in the laager's surrender:

> At daybreak, Kaiser, secretary to General Cronje, went over to British lines with white flag with the offer to surrender, no conditions asked. As he was passing where I was standing he said, 'This day's work costs us the Independence of the Transvaal'. Shortly he returns

British troops survey the destruction of Cronje's wagon laager at Paardeberg.

again to bring Cronje himself. The General rides over on horseback, dressed in topcoat, big wide awake hat, and the inevitable big riding whip (with which he has laced many a burgher). On passing he gave orders that white flags were to be put up at distances of a hundred yards all along trenches on this side.

As John Moody Lane was taken prisoner, he may well have been led past L. March Phillipps, who experienced mixed feelings on being brought face to face with the enemy:

> I was one of a party that rode down with the Major on the morning of the surrender to the laager and saw the prisoners marched in. They seemed quite cheery and pleased with themselves. They were dressed in all sorts of ragged, motley-looking clothes; trousers of cheap tweed, such as you see hung up in an East End slop-shop; jackets once black, now rusted, torn and stained, and battered hats. They reminded one more of a mob of Kent hop-pickers than anything else, and it was a matter of some surprise, not to say disgust, to some of us to think that such a sorry crowd should be able to withstand disciplined troops in the way they did.

Nineteen years earlier, to the day, the Boers had won the first Anglo-Boer War at Majuba Hill. In this second conflict, the Battle of Paardeberg marked a turning point in the fortunes of the Boers. In what was one of the most serious reverses of the war, 4,000 fighting men were lost at a stroke. Cronje and his wife were packed off to a prisoner of war camp on the island of St Helena and, as Christiaan de Wet later wrote, the news of Cronje's surrender had a palpable effect on the Boers left fighting in the field:

> No words can describe my feelings…depression and discouragement were written on every face. The effects of this blow, it is not too much to say, made themselves apparent to the very end of the war.

For the Boers, the surrender of Cronje and 4,000 of his men was one of the most serious reverses of the war.

At the same time that an old grievance was being 'wiped off the slate' at Paardeberg, Sir Redvers Buller was once again fighting his way across the Tugela River. This time Buller took a different approach. He pushed forward his entire force in one movement so that the Boers were fully occupied all the way down their lines. As the infantry attacked, the artillery was used to provide a

*Boer prisoners of war were deported to places like Ceylon,
and St Helena whose most famous inhabitant had
been Napoleon. They remained there for the duration
of the war.*

'creeping barrage' so that their entire advance was covered by a bombardment perhaps only 100 metres in front of them. By developing a broad strategy that encompassed a series of engagements over a number of days instead of one set-piece battle, Buller finally managed to overcome Louis Botha's force and made his way across the plains to Ladysmith.

Ladysmith had by this time been besieged for over three months, and the Boers' most effective weapons – starvation and disease – were taking their toll. Drummer H. Goodwin was part of the British garrison and was moved to write bitterly of his experience:

When Ladysmith was first besieged, the civilians stowed all their food away and poor Tommy Atkins that is the soldier's name starved with them. But what was the result when Ladysmith ran short? They did not share with poor Tommy. If anyone saw Ladysmith they would want to know what we are fighting for. It is a miserable looking place and don't forget it has a fat graveyard with our poor lads but I hope that they are better off out of the misery of a life such as this.

As the food shortage had progressively worsened, the garrison was forced to eat its own cavalry horses. When the town residents were eventually put on army rations, it was clear that Sir George White was expecting the siege to drag on. Corporal James Cowland noted the effect that the siege conditions were having on his fellow soldiers:

Things are looking very black now and the best of us can't help feeling a trifle disheartened. Rations are shortened again by one half, i.e. 'mealie' pap and the usual ration of horseflesh…It is quite pitiful to see the state of some poor fellows crawling about with not an atom of strength in them, looking hungry and care-worn, and nearly all suffering from the terrible dysentery caused principally by the bad water, which the Boers have done their best to pollute with dead carcasses.

With so many men and horses in an enclosed area, dysentery and enteric fever swept through the garrison. Hospital records from the siege show that there were 10,673 admissions to hospital from a garrison of 13,497. Although there were three field hospitals in the town, most typhoid sufferers were sent to Intombi camp – a train ride away in no man's land. Originally built to house 300, within three months Intombi was trying to cope with almost 2,000 victims of the disease epidemic. Starved of medicines and staff, the death rate by January had risen to between ten and twenty per day.

Unlike Mafeking and Kimberley, Ladysmith was populated predominantly by a fully armed field force. It was ironic, then, that the main activity throughout the siege was not fighting but waiting. The monotony of the day-to-day situation tended to give any news from the outside a heightened significance. It was not surprising that the succession of hopeful heliographs followed all too quickly by news of another reverse had badly dented the town's morale. The *Argus* correspondent Donald MacDonald had been filing dispatches for some weeks describing the fighting around Ladysmith:

In Natal war was divested of absolutely everything that once lent it meretricious glamour – no bright uniforms, no inspiring bands playing men into battle, no flags, no glitter or smoke or circumstance of any kind, but just plain primeval killing, without redemption, and with every advantage taken that international law allows.

On 28 February the message came through from Buller that the garrison had been expecting for four months:

Have thoroughly beaten the enemy. Believe them to be in full retreat. Have sent my cavalry to ascertain which way they have gone.

The garrison lookouts strained all afternoon to catch sight of Buller's forces. As word spread, people had rushed down to the town gates. Corporal James Cowland made a note of what happened next:

There was great excitement about 7.30 p.m. when a body of horsemen were seen approaching the town from the direction of Intombi Spruit. In answer to the challenge 'Who goes there?' the welcome answer came back 'Ladysmith Relief Force'. Then ensued a scene of indescribable excitement and enthusiasm. We were all running about like mad, kissing and laughing and crying by turns, such was the depth of our feelings.

At a cost of more than 5,500 men, the British army in Natal had finally relieved Ladysmith. Sir George White, who through his initial strategic blunder had brought about the 118-day siege, made an emotional speech thanking God they had 'kept the flag flying'. The flag may have still been flying, but his reputation was in tatters and he was invalided home to England shortly afterwards.

As Buller relaxed at Ladysmith after a triumphal procession into the town, Private Thomas Cook noted in his diary:

We was all glad about Ladysmith being relieved and the capture of Cronje & all his men. That ought to dishearten them a bit.

The Boers were indeed disheartened. Within just two weeks they had lost two of the three main siege towns, the bulk of their army in the west and any prospect of mounting more offensives in Natal. The British were holding their own in the Cape midlands, and now the capital of the Orange Free State was under threat from Lord Roberts and his 30,000 men.

As burghers streamed back to their farms, the

Above: *The reversal of Boer fortunes precipitated a series of crisis meetings among the Republican leadership to stem the tide of burghers returning to their farms.*
Right: *When the British finally relieved Ladysmith in February 1900, Sir George White declared 'I thank God we have kept the flag flying.'*

CAVALRY ENTERING LADYSMITH COPYRIG

The First Shell
Ladysmith, November 1899

two Boer Presidents, Kruger and Steyn, could see their forces disintegrating around them, and after a crisis conference at Bloemfontein Kruger rode down to rally the burghers at Poplar Grove. The 6,000 men under Christiaan de Wet and the 6,000 or so reinforcements who were being pulled back from Natal and the Cape represented the last realistic chance the Boers had of stopping Roberts' advance from Paardeberg to Bloemfontein. Shortly after Kruger entered De Wet's tent on 7 March the two men heard the sound of firing and rushed out to see what was going on.

Coincidentally, 7 March was also the day that Roberts decided to resume his march. Fully cognizant of the Boers' presence at Poplar Grove, he

Above: *For the inhabitants of Ladysmith, the panic caused by random shelling soon gave way to intense boredom, and frustration at the British Army's repeated failure to break through Boer lines.*
Opposite: *The relief of Ladysmith caused scenes like this one in London to be played out across Britain.*

had devised a plan drawing on the lessons that had been learned at Paardeberg. General French and the cavalry would ride around the Boers' east side and cut off their escape to Bloemfontein. A division of infantry would push them towards the Modder River and then another two divisions would attack them from the front and from the far river bank.

The problem for Roberts was that the Boers had also learned a lesson at Paardeberg, and as soon as they were given the merest hint of a possible encirclement they hitched up their wagons and ran like the wind. French's horses had been ridden into the ground and were in no condition to mount an effective pursuit; the infantry had been on half-rations since the transport fiasco at Waterval Drift and they, too, did not have the energy to halt the fleeing Boers. Roberts was bitterly disappointed. He had to watch, powerless, as De Wet, all his men and, as he later discovered, President Kruger got clean away. There were mutual recriminations between Roberts and French that such a gift of an opportunity had been lost.

As a stream of wagons thundered panic-stricken towards Bloemfontein, Kruger and De la Rey, who had been on his way down with more men, were powerless to stop them. They had halted at a place called Abraham's Kraal near Driefontein and decided that De la Rey should try to detain Roberts here while Kruger and Steyn used the extra time to prepare the defences in Bloemfontein.

Roberts had split his men into three columns 16 kilometres apart, and they resumed their laborious progress through the Orange Free State. When French, who was leading the first column, spotted De la Rey's presence at Abraham's Kraal, he attempted to skirt round him to the south. But De la Rey had planned for this, and French ended up riding straight into the Boer lines at Driefontein. In an all-too-familiar scene, 1,500 Boers managed to keep 10,000 Khakis at bay for an entire day. It was only when a creeping artillery barrage enabled the infantry to launch an overwhelming assault that the Boers, still firing to the last moment, were forced to flee.

Roberts completed his march to Bloemfontein unimpeded, and the town was entered on the morning of 13 March by three journalists who just

happened to get there first. It seemed that the recent crop of failures had broken the Boers' spirit, and they had left Bloemfontein for the British to take unopposed. The Free State archives were moved to Kroonstad and President Steyn boarded a train out of the capital. By early afternoon, a silk Union Jack made for him by his wife, Nora, had been run up the flagpole by Lord Roberts.

As the weary procession marched down the attractive main street of Bloemfontein, people

This ceremony at Bloemfontein marked the annexation of the Orange Free State and its new name – the Orange River Colony.

cheered and waved Union Jacks. It somehow did not feel like the capture of the enemy's capital. The men were looking forward to a slice of normal life after over a month's hard slog with no let-up. Rest, relaxation and some much-missed female company were on their minds.

Unfortunately, their stay at Bloemfontein was not to be as pleasant as they had hoped. Dr Kay de Villiers, a medical historian brought up in the Free State, explains why:

Short of transport, short of men, short of supplies, fighting major battles, they come as victors to Bloemfontein. An old lady – she was then ninety-two – told me that as a little girl, her impressions of this marching army entering Bloemfontein were firstly the

monotony of the fife and the drum and secondly how tired they looked. And the child was right, but they were not tired, they were tired and sick. And she could see it. And that army lands 30,000 people in Bloemfontein, which was a small town then, and within six weeks there were more than 5,000 people with typhoid.

Typhoid, or enteric fever as it was called, was not a new disease to the British. It was spread by contaminated drinking water and there had been several epidemics in England, the most recent at Blackburn in 1881, Worthing in 1893 and Maidstone in 1897. The War Office had already discovered how poor the general health of the population was when it had to turn down large numbers of volunteers after Black Week. Roberts' men were prime candidates for the disease: with inadequate supplies of clean water, they lived closely together in unsanitary conditions and would camp for days at a time near already polluted water sources:

Certainly when the British army was lying at Modder River Station, the chances are that that water was already contaminated with typhoid. If you took a large body of

Previous page: The typhoid epidemic at Bloemfontein was caused by the British troops, vulnerable to the disease, drinking and bathing in the polluted Modder River.
Right: *For Captain L. March Phillipps parts of the Modder River looked not dissimilar to Bovril.*

BOVRIL

AT THE FRONT & IN THE FRONT

people like that army coming from Britain, there could have been a few typhoid-carriers there as well.

Dr de Villiers puts the Bloemfontein typhoid epidemic down to the soldiers' prolonged stay at the Modder River. The men suffering from dysentery even referred to it as 'a dose of the Modders', and L. March Phillipps was under no illusions about the quality of the water they were drinking and washing in:

The river, more muddy than ever, moves languidly in its deep channel. There is a Boer laager some miles above the camp, the scourings of which – horrid thought! – are constantly brought down to us. The soldiers eye the infected current askance and call it *Boervril*. Its effect is seen in the sickness that is steadily increasing.

That sickness was not confined to the British. After being forced to live surrounded by rotting carcasses and their own waste, many of the 4,000 prisoners from Cronje's laager at Paardeberg were also brought down by typhoid and dysentery.

The military authorities were aware of the dangers of contaminated water – officers were provided with filters – but, as Dr de Villiers explains, the difficulty was in finding an effective way of dealing with it:

They warned the people and they said drink filter water, drink boiled water, but the men seemed not to care. They had to put a sentry out to prevent them drinking the water. Thirst is a terrible thing. It's dry, it's dusty, it's very hot, and they've marched and they're thirsty. Who now has the inclination to ladle out a bit of water, boil it, have it cooled and then drink it? Perhaps the Boer chap who almost habitually drank only coffee and not water was safer because his water was at least boiled for his coffee.

So the men who marched into Bloemfontein on 13 March were incubating typhoid. Within days or even hours, the town's water supply was contaminated and the soldiers started dropping like flies. Because of the transport situation, medical supplies had been cut to a minimum. There were very few trained staff, and the few field hospitals that there were contained stretchers rather than beds. The Royal Army Medical Corps did their best to deal with the unprecedented scale of sickness, but requests for more supplies to be sent up fell on stony ground.

> Every available building that could serve as a hospital in Bloemfontein was co-opted into the service as a hospital, but what do you do, where do you get staff from, the utensils and the various bits of apparatus that you need to treat people who are terribly sick? Someone spoke to Kitchener about this and his response was: 'You want pills and I want bullets, and bullets come first.'

The result of this complete abdication of responsibility by the military authorities was that by the end of April almost a thousand troops who had entered the town only a month earlier had died of typhoid in Bloemfontein:

> And they died miserably, they really did. Feverish, dehydrated, diarrhoea, haemorrhaging, a dry foul mouth, delirious, extreme headache, it was not pleasant, it is not a kind disease.

This would be the last war in which more troops died from diseases than from wounds inflicted by the enemy. Out of the 21,000 British deaths in South Africa, only 8,000 were attributable to wounds on the battlefield. Private C. Ireland wrote:

> At this place we shortly knew the danger soldiers have to put up with on service. Our men were carried by threes and fours to be attended by doctors for dysentery. Every afternoon we could see fourteen or fifteen funerals at the cemetery gates.

The enforced six-week stay at Bloemfontein enabled both sides to take stock of the situation. Roberts issued a proclamation offering an amnesty to every Free State burgher, except the leaders, who laid down his arms and signed the oath of allegiance. He then concentrated on reopening the waterworks and the railway running south. As the number of British and colonial troops in South Africa reached 210,000, the War Office poured in more supplies and replenished the decimated cavalry. During March and April, 18,000 horses and 11,260 mules were either shipped almost 10,000 kilometres from Britain or bought locally. After the railway was put back into action, boots, uniforms, ammunition and guns were all sent up by the trainload as plans were made for the march to the Transvaal capital, Pretoria.

Meanwhile, the Boers, with no such resources available to them, held a council of war in the temporary Free State capital of Kroonstad. It seemed clear to Christiaan de Wet that mobility was the key in the struggle against such overwhelming British manpower. It was equally clear that the amount of impedimenta accompanying many of the burghers fighting in the field was a serious hindrance to that mobility. The disaster at Paardeberg had occurred because Cronje was slowed down by an enormous wagon laager. The council of war agreed that wagon camps would be dispensed with, allowing the Boer forces to carry out the 'hit-and-run' tactics at which they excelled.

The plan was not to defeat the British militarily; such a disparity in numbers made that almost inconceivable. Rather, the Boers would wear the British down, cut their communications and supply lines and generally harass them as much as possible. Such a strategy was the Boers' best chance of persuading other European powers to press for a negotiated peace. President Kruger also counted on the hand of God to come to the aid of his people. Although they had lost about 10,000 men since October 1899, there were still enough men in the field to make this a workable plan. Mafeking was still under siege, commandos were placed in the Biggarsberg mountains and Van Reenen's Pass to stop Buller from breaking through into the Transvaal or the Orange Free State from Natal, and the hope remained that a rebellion could be raised among the Afrikaners in the Cape Colony.

The other problem addressed at the March council of war was that of absenteeism. While the British forces were succumbing to typhoid and dysentery, the plague currently depleting the Boer forces was the one they called leave-pest. It was clear that strict regulations would need to be enforced to stop the burghers from nipping off home whenever their crops needed harvesting or when things were getting a little warm on the battlefield.

Along with a refinement of Boer operations came a change in their leadership. Until now the war had been conducted by older generals. But the Transvaal burgher Roland Schikkerling wrote:

Our particular case required men, alert, impetuous and capable of endurance. The older officers were a drag on our skipping spirits.

With the capture of Cronje in February and the death of General Joubert in March, the field was open to younger, more dynamic men. Louis Botha replaced Joubert to take command of the Transvaal forces, and Christiaan de Wet took charge of the Free State forces. De Wet showed particular insight when he sent his burghers home on a fortnight's leave with an arrangement to regroup at Sand River on 25 March. After all, he explained to a sceptical Joubert, 'I cannot catch a hare with unwilling dogs'.

The burghers who came back were inevitably fewer than those who had gone, but what they lacked in numbers they made up for in renewed enthusiasm for the task ahead of them. De Wet soon showed Roberts that the Free Staters would not give up that easily.

The most vivid example of the renewed Boer spirit happened just six days after De Wet's men had regrouped. The Bloemfontein waterworks were situated 37 kilometres east of the town at a place called Sannah's Post. On 31 March De Wet not only succeeded in cutting off Bloemfontein's water supply, which immediately worsened the typhoid epidemic, but also managed to ambush a passing British cavalry force, inflicting losses of 600 men, eighty out of ninety wagons and seven out of twelve guns. To have achieved this practically under the nose of the Commander-in-Chief and his 30,000 men persuaded many of the burghers who had signed the oath of allegiance to bring back out the weapons they had carefully hidden away from the eyes of the British.

During April, De Wet was able to pull off two more daring raids to the south of Bloemfontein. On 4 April he attacked the Royal Irish Rifles at Reddersburg, managing to effect the surrender of the entire garrison and the capture of 546 men.

General Louis Botha breathed new life into the Transvaal forces after the death of General Joubert.

HOEPEN's
TO

Later in the month he went for a garrison containing 1,900 men of Brabant's Horse. What De Wet and his men found particularly appealing about this target was that they were mainly Cape Afrikaners who had volunteered for five shillings a day to fight for the Queen. Despite the fact that he was unable to break them, it was with particular relish that De Wet laid siege to them for sixteen days. By the time Roberts' men had lumbered to the scene with reinforcements, De Wet and his flying column were long gone.

De Wet's raids in April were just an indication of the lightning strikes that would plague the British throughout the rest of the war and a taste of the difficulty they would have in catching him.

By 3 May Roberts was finally ready to resume his march to Pretoria. Despite leaving behind the 4,500 men who were too sick to travel, the column was an impressive sight, as L. March Phillipps recorded:

> Endless battalions of infantry, very dusty and grimy, but going light and strong; guns, bearer companies, Colonial Horse, generals and their staffs, go plodding and jingling by in a procession that seems to be going on forever. And beside and through them the long convoys of the different units, in heavy masses, come groaning and creaking along, the oxen sweating, the dust whirling, the naked Kaffirs yelling, and the long whips going like pistol-shots. The whole thing suggests more a national migration than the march of an army.

As Roberts concerned himself with the 480-kilometre hike to Pretoria, there was still a little matter that needed to be cleared up in the north. Although the military authorities did not seem to be unduly worried by it, the siege that had perhaps most captured the British public's imagination was still continuing in Mafeking. Newspapers, including young Arthur Whitlock's *Daily Mail*, were full of the bravery of the little town and the heroism of the man in charge.

> Baden-Powell, he was held up as one of the highest images really and we almost worshipped him, I should say more so than we did Buller, and he became a national hero to us.

Although his popularity was widespread at home, Baden-Powell's stock in Mafeking was not universally high. *The Times* correspondent Angus Hamilton was often quite critical of the way the siege was being handled, an attitude that resulted in most of his dispatches ending up in the censor's wastebasket. The stories that were allowed out concentrated on the plucky stoicism of the inhabitants, but in reality that stoicism was wearing a little thin. As long ago as January, the Barolong interpreter Sol Plaatje had written in his diary:

> Another shell burst in the south; we wonder how long this is going to last. Instead of getting brighter, the prospect in front of us is darkening…I am inclined to believe that the Boers have fully justified their bragging, for we are citizens of a town of subjects of the richest and the strongest empire on earth and the burghers of a small state have successfully besieged us for three months.

There was also an increasing amount of tension between Baden-Powell and the Barolong chief, Wessels. While he was happy for his people to work with the British in the interests of preserving their own security, he trusted the British as little as he trusted the Boers. According to Angus Hamilton, Wessels told the Barolongs that:

> …the English wished to make slaves of them; that they would not be paid for any services rendered; nor…would they be given any food, but left to starve when the critical moment came.

Although Wessels was soon suspended from his chieftaincy for what Baden-Powell described as 'want of energy', his words did seem to have an element of truth to them. The very Africans who had constructed all the defence works, who were being sent out on cattle-raiding expeditions and who were gathering intelligence were also the ones who were being affected most acutely by the shortage of food. As Sol Plaatje recorded, when food became a problem, it was the African rations that Baden-Powell cut first:

There is a proclamation by the Colonel R. S. S. Baden Powell that no food stores of any kind would in future be sold to the public; and white people are now going to buy food in rations and be compelled to buy small

The black people of Mafeking often had their own food supplies commandeered and then sold back to them by the military authorities.

quantities, the same as blacks. I have often heard the black folks say money is useless as you cannot eat it when you are hungry, and now I have seen it and experienced it. The thing appears to be going from bad to worse.

As early as December 1899, the effects of the food shortage on some of the Africans were vividly apparent to nurse Ina Cowan:

The Kaffirs dig up dead horses and eat them, and sit and pick on the rubbish heaps. Some of them are starving. I have seen as many dreadful things as I ever wish to see.

Unfortunately, Nurse Cowan would have to witness many more dreadful things as Baden-Powell continued to diminish both the quality and the quantity of black rations to sustain a decent level for the whites.

When Baden-Powell was made aware of the fact that there were people actually dying of starvation, he set up a soup kitchen and extreme cases were officially entitled to free servings. But everyone else had to pay for their serving, and the soup kitchen was run at a profit. James Marumo's grandmother lived in the native stadt at Mafeking:

Because they were surrounded, there was no food, they lived on soup, which was cooked in big pots, and at a certain time they would take their cups and go and get served…you would keep the soup and you would sleep having only that soup. They lost weight, their eyes were protruding outwards. She said that when they wanted to increase this soup, they went to the river and took mud and ate it, so at last there would be something in their stomachs.

To ease the situation Baden-Powell decided not to decrease the white rations, for who knew how long the town might be besieged, but rather to 'persuade' the 2,000 refugees to leave Mafeking. The persuasion B-P had in mind was a basic carrot-and-stick approach to the problem. He arranged for Colonel Plumer to lay down food supplies 110 kilometres away in Bechuanaland and closed the grain stores to the refugees in Mafeking. The hopelessness of the refugees' situation was not lost on Edward Ross, an auctioneer in Mafeking:

Very hard luck on them, having no choice but that of two deaths, one being shot by Dutchmen, or that of

As food became increasingly scarce, horseflesh was added to the rations but the soup kitchens were still run at a profit.

staying here to slowly starve to death.

A group of 700 Barolong women tried to break through the Boer lines in early April but only ten succeeded and the rest were forced to return to Mafeking, some of them having been physically abused. Later in the month a group of 200 did manage to cross the lines unscathed, but days later nine women from a group of thirteen were shot.

Extract from the Diary of a Baby in Mafeking. 1900.
"It isn't so much the shells that I object to; It is this Everlasting standing on one's head while Mother does her washing."

The most severe cases of starvation were among the 2,000 refugees who had come to Mafeking at the start of the war. They were a mixture of people, and relations between them and the resident Barolongs plummeted as food became increasingly scarce. J. Emerson Neilly, the correspondent for the *Pall Mall Gazette*, was moved to write:

> I saw them fall down on the veld and lie where they had fallen, too weak to go on their way. The sufferers were mostly little boys – mere infants ranging from four or five upwards...Probably hundreds died from starvation or the diseases that always accompany famine...Words could not portray the scene of misery; five or six hundred human frameworks of both sexes and all ages...standing in lines, each holding an old blackened can or beef tin, awaiting turn to crawl painfully up to the soup kitchen...It was one of the most heart-rending sights I have ever witnessed.

The policy of trying to reduce the number of Africans in Makefing was in some degree successful, although it was predominantly Barolongs who left and refugees who stayed. The food shortage

was relieved to such an extent by their departure that Baden-Powell could even consider *increasing* the white rations, as his diary entry shows:

> Ap 20: Meat and meal stocks at present will last to June 12. But by forcing Natives away from Mafeking we can get their share of horseflesh for whites and their sowen [a gruel made with grain husks] which would improve the [white] ration in size.

Colonel Plumer received just over 1,200 people who had made the journey from Mafeking, and by the first week of May three-quarters of the Barolong stadt had left. This was in part due to the fact that the Boers had reduced the number of men encircling Mafeking, making it easier for people to leave unharmed.

While the food shortage was never life-threatening for the white population, the situation was serious nevertheless, and people endured great privations during a siege that would last twice as long as those of Kimberley and Ladysmith. Ethne Bernard's mother regularly had to queue for food:

> One of the stories my mother told me was standing in a queue at hospital to get a quarter of a pound of maize flour, for her baby sister Doris. And while she was there she heard firing, gunfire from the north, and she was terrified and wanted to run home, but realized she had to stand her ground otherwise baby Doris wouldn't have anything to eat...Only later when she

Many of Eloff's burghers were trapped by the Barolongs as they tried to enter Mafeking through the native stad.

got home and then they realized that it wasn't enemy firing in the north, it was the relief column coming in. But unfortunately that baby sister that she stood there to get the mazzina for, didn't survive the siege. She was obviously not well nourished and as a small child ate sand, handfuls of sand and eventually she died.

It was as Roberts prepared for his march to Pretoria that he received a note from Baden-Powell informing him of the seriousness of the food situation in Mafeking. A flying column, 2,000 strong, was dispatched from near Kimberley led by Colonel Mahon and consisting mainly of South African volunteers. The plan was to join hands with Colonel Plumer's Rhodesian Mounted Regiment and some Canadian reinforcements and to overpower the Boers who remained around Mafeking.

As Plumer and Mahon made their way towards each other, Sarel Eloff, Kruger's grandson, had other ideas. After being told by Kruger that he must take the town at all costs, he devised a daring plan and managed to persuade his slightly reluctant superior, General Snyman, to go along with it.

Eloff and about 700 men would enter the town through the native stad, pausing only to set the little huts on fire. The flames would scare the Barolongs and act as a signal for Snyman to gallop in with reinforcements and take Mafeking.

Under cover of darkness on 12 May, Eloff and a disappointing turnout of only 240 men successfully pierced the outer defences and set fire to the stadt. The Barolongs managed to trap a good proportion of the Boers in the cattle kraals, but Eloff had made it through and captured Colonel Hore's garrison located just 400 metres from the town itself.

The flames from the stad had alerted Snyman but they had also alerted Baden-Powell, and at the frantic ringing of the church bells the townspeople leaped out of bed and armed themselves. Even the prisoners in the local jail were given weapons. Snyman's belated and completely inadequate attempt to get in to Mafeking was easily repulsed. The tables had been turned on Eloff and from entering the garrison as the besieger he quickly became the besieged. After a day of waiting for Snyman, he was forced to surrender to the prisoners he had taken that morning.

If Snyman had risen to the occasion, Eloff's plan could well have worked, but as it was the Boers lost 108 men as prisoners and another sixty were dead or wounded. The fatalities would have been a lot higher had it not been for a British officer stepping in to prevent the Barolongs avenging

After eight months under siege, the heliographers at Mafeking could finally signal 'welcome' to the relief column.

themselves on the Boers still held captive in the kraal. The British casualties amounted to twelve dead and eight wounded. Most of those were the Africans who were widely acknowledged to have saved the day.

It would take another five days before Ethne Bernard's mother would hear the approach of the relief column. Mahon and Plumer, after joining hands, had to fend off 2,000 men under Koos de la Rey, who had been sent by Botha to try to salvage the situation. As they rode to a Mafeking full of people standing on roofs trying to see them, Mahon heliographed: 'How are you getting on?' Baden-Powell, after seven months of siege, simply replied: 'Welcome.'

The understated tone of the heliographs was not reflected in the response of the public when

the news reached Britain. Minnie Way remembers what happened in Scotland:

> The relief of Mafeking – oh, that was a happy night in Glasgow. My mother said the whole theatre that night just emptied and everybody ran to the public house for a drink. They were that happy to know there would be some men come home from Mafeking.

And if the *Handsworth Herald* is to be believed, the response in Birmingham was even more euphoric:

> Staid citizens, whose severe respectability and decorum were usually beyond question or reproach, were to be seen parading the streets, shouting patriotic songs with the full force of their lungs, dancing, jumping, screaming in a delirium of unrestrained joy.

This unprecedented taking to the streets would outstrip even the reactions at the end of the First and Second World Wars. A new word entered the dictionaries, as the humorist Saki demonstrated in his couplet:

> Mother, may I go and 'maffick',
> Tear around and hinder traffic?

In the public's eyes the relief of Mafeking stood for far more than the rescue of a relatively insignificant border town. This was a triumph of 'Britishness' – of pluck, of resourcefulness, of humour in the face of adversity. The lifting of the sieges also acted as a release valve after the defeats and humiliations of Black Week and Spion Kop. Arthur Whitlock remembers:

> As these various places were relieved – Kimberley and so on – there was a great response of the people here. But I think most of all it was when we came to the final one of Mafeking, when there was a tremendous outcry of joy among the people there. There was shouting in the streets and suchlike and all the newspapers were full of that, particularly the *Daily Mail*…It was a time of very great rejoicing. And we thought we'd turned the corner then.

The *Daily Mail*, along with the rest of the popular press, had stirred up an interest in Mafeking that far surpassed the other siege towns, but the newspapers were ably helped in this by the figure

Above: *The 13th battalion of the Imperial Yeomanry were dealt a humiliating blow by Piet de Wet.*
Left: *The relief of 'gallant little Mafeking' gave Lord Roberts' men a much needed burst of energy on their long march north.*

of Baden-Powell. He was so popular that even a month before the relief, Major Alick Godley, who was Baden-Powell's right-hand man, wrote to his wife:

> At the music halls in London, the Cinematograph produces portraits of Roberts, Kitchener, Buller, Kruger, Joubert which are cheered or hissed, and they used to include B-P, but now they have had to put him separately at the end and exhibit him for about six encores; they have to wait for about twenty minutes or half an hour for the cheering to abate before they can play 'God Save the Queen'.

As one would expect, the situation was not quite as clear cut in Mafeking itself. For the Barolongs this was not *the* siege of Mafeking, as they had been besieged by the Boers six times before, once for two years. Neither did their suffering end with the appearance of Mahon and Plumer. Because of the decision to disarm the Africans immediately after the lifting of the siege, the Barolongs were left completely defenceless against attacks by armed Boers still in the area.

The contribution of the Barolongs in defending Mafeking for seven months was never acknowledged by the British. When in June B-P requested that he be allowed to give war medals to some of the Barolong leaders, Roberts responded:

> A signed parchment would probably be as much appreciated as a war medal and would avoid the suggestion that we had armed natives.

At a Royal Commission in 1903, Baden-Powell would not only deny that he had armed Africans but would insult the brave men who had fought for him, saying that when he tried to make them defend their town they had all run away at the first attack.

The relief of Mafeking was symbolic for the Boers. It was the place from which Jameson had begun his raid. For it to have been relieved by many of those same Uitlanders who had precipitated this war added another layer of bitterness. Taking strength from his faith, Louis Botha sent round a circular the following day:

> With a view to the grave state of the country in these anxious times, a state which the almighty has brought upon us as a necessary trial, a state from which we all hope to emerge purified, and from which we shall also emerge stronger, more vigorous and finer provided we believe in him only and forcibly banish all hypocritical faith, I deem it necessary and good to proclaim tomorrow a general day of humiliation.

The sieges of Ladysmith, Kimberley and Mafeking, with their twin motifs of shelling and starvation, had been miserable episodes for the people trapped inside the towns. They had also exacted a heavy cost on the British forces trying to relieve them. While it is undeniable that the sieges determined the course of the first six months of the war, Janice Farquharson does not rate their significance very highly.

> Of the sieges, Ladysmith should have been decisive. But there were these old men on both sides bumbling around, not doing anything, not getting anywhere, it was a thorough cock-up. Kimberley and Mafeking are different. Kimberley, again a clash of personalities, but apart from the diamonds, it had no significance. Rhodes' abounding egotism also provided motivation. Mafeking was an exercise in management and exhibitionism by Baden-Powell, and indecision on the part of the Boers. But really they were all so damned silly and so unnecessary.

Silly and unnecessary they may have been, but the sieges raised two issues that became increasingly important as the war progressed. Firstly, the suffering of the Africans was equal to, and often greater than, that of the whites. Sometimes this was unavoidable; sometimes it was deliberate policy. Secondly, from almost the first shot being fired, civilians were seen as legitimate targets, and the war did not restrict itself to the two combatant armies.

Lord Roberts proceeded north towards Pretoria. He had decided not to deal with De Wet before leaving the Free State (which was officially annexed by the Crown on 28 May and called the Orange River Colony) for a number of reasons. One of those reasons was that he had been sent word that the Boers were about to destroy the mines in Johannesburg. This would be disastrous not just for European big business but also for the British Treasury, which was footing the bill for Roberts' current expedition. Another reason for not delaying his entry into the Transvaal any longer was that Roberts felt sure that the psychological effects of losing their capitals and most of their major towns would break the Boers' resolve to carry on. The hope was that his march would draw the main body of the enemy towards him, when he would crush them once and for all.

The numerical superiority of the British was overwhelming, and the sight of tens of thousands of men marching steadily and inevitably towards the Boer capital was a fearsome sight. Ada Prinsloo remembers her mother's description of the sheer numbers facing the commandos:

> My mother often told us that as [the English columns] came marching towards them, it really looked as though the earth was trembling. When an English soldier fell in battle and died, or was shot dead, the others would simply climb over them and carry on coming. It was actually a hopeless case and a hopeless task for the Boers to carry on fighting. I mean, for the Boers to even think of winning the war.

The best that the Boers could do was to send a detachment to snap at the heels of the advancing columns, while the remainder briskly retreated north with their wagons and guns.

While it was demoralizing to be herded through the Free State like sheep, it was equally frustrating for the British cavalry, who were constantly being denied the opportunity to 'get stuck in'.

As fast as Roberts went, the Boers were always one step ahead of him. Private Thomas Cook, who was following in Roberts' wake, gave some idea of the pace of the march in his diary entry for 24 May:

> My own birthday but not much of a one. We marched again at 8 a.m. Marched 15 miles & no halt again. I believe the old pig is trying to kill us. I should think we should get treated better if we had one of the Boers in charge of us. All our volunteers swear that they would never come up again & they have only been with us one month so we will leave you to guess what it's like.

Roberts' force swept northwards along the railway, through the temporary Boer capital of Kroonstad and on until they came to Doornkop, two hours' ride from Johannesburg. It was here that Jameson had surrendered, and it was here that the Boers had entrenched in a last-ditch attempt to save the City of Gold.

As French took 3,000 troops to outflank the Boers to the west, the Gordon Highlanders launched a frontal assault on the ridge. Charging up the hill without artillery cover, the Gordons took up their positions opposite the Boer lines. Then in open order, line after line, they walked towards the enemy's fire. Bayonets were fixed and the hill was taken. It was an astonishing display of bravery later to be described as carrying on the 'glorious traditions of the British infantry'. It also cost the Gordons a hundred men in ten minutes. The

less glittering aspect of this high military ideal faced L. March Phillipps as he rode out the next day:

Lord Roberts' delayed march into Johannesburg allowed the Boers to escape with a significant amount of gold.

> Next morning at dawn, escorting the cow-guns, I came to where the Boers had held out so long among the scattered rocks. The Gordons were burying some of the Boer dead. There were several quite youngsters among them. One was a boy of not more than fourteen, I should think, like an English schoolboy. One of the Gordons there told me he saw him, during the advance, kneeling behind a stone and firing. He was shot through the forehead. There is something pathetic and infinitely disagreeable in finding these mere children opposed to one.

The Battle of Doornkop opened the door to Johannesburg and, after a twenty-four-hour delay in which Roberts agreed to let all the Boers escape before entering, the city was his. With hindsight it could be said that this decision resulted in the war dragging on for another two years. At the time, though, Roberts thought it the most effective way of preserving the mines, and he was still confident of a Boer collapse when he took Pretoria.

On 31 May the British marched into Johannesburg. Lord Kerry, Roberts' aide-de-camp, wrote a blunt description of the scene:

> A good many people all along the road chiefly niggers and jews, and a big crowd waiting outside the law courts, unattractive looking people speaking with

tongues, mostly friendly and wearing red white and blue badges but an occasional groan could be heard.

If the Africans on the streets thought that the arrival of Lord Roberts would improve their situation, they were about to be disappointed. Rather than taking the opportunity to demonstrate Britain's stated desire to improve the lot of the native, Roberts' military government demonstrated instead its deeply held commitment to keeping the wages of the mine-boys as low as possible. The restrictive pass laws and the prohibition against walking on the pavement were not altered.

Roberts' crowning glory was in his grasp. Pretoria was only 65 kilometres away, and on 3 June he embarked on the last leg of his journey. When he was only halfway there he received reports of a mass exodus from the city. It looked as though Pretoria was to be left undefended as well.

After a slight delay at the hands of Koos de la Rey, Roberts entered Pretoria on 5 June and once again produced the silk Union Jack made by his wife to run up the flagpole. Although no one could dispute the speed and ease with which the 480-kilometre march had been completed, L. March Phillips expressed the sense of anticlimax which accompanied yet another interminable procession into a city devoid of the enemy:

> It is generally considered rather a coup in war, I believe, to take the enemy's capital, isn't it? Like taking a queen at chess. We keep on taking capitals, but I can't see it seems to make much difference. The Boers set no store by them apparently; neither Bloemfontein nor Pretoria have been seriously defended, and they go on fighting after their loss just as if nothing had happened.

The lowering of the Transvaal flag at Pretoria marked the beginning of a new phase of the war.

*By the end of the war more than 30,000 Boer farms had
been burned by the British.*

CHAPTER FIVE

Ungentlemanly Conduct

Last Wednesday we took a farm house. The men bolted but the women we took to our camp. Then we smashed the furniture up and burnt it. There were two nice pianos in the house. We played 'God Save the King' and smashed them to pieces with the rest of the furniture, beds and everything. It did seem a pity.

PERCY DAY WRITING HOME TO HIS MOTHER

A T THE BEGINNING OF June 1900 there was no doubt that the Boer leadership of the Transvaal was seriously demoralized. On 1 June President Steyn of the Free State was angered at receiving a telegram from Kruger suggesting immediate surrender. Along with Louis Botha and Jan Smuts, Kruger had seen an increasingly steady stream of burghers laying down their arms and returning to their farms. In fact the situation was so bad that March to July of that year saw the surrender of forty per cent of the burghers who had been mobilized at the outbreak of war. For Kruger, there was simply no prospect of defending Pretoria with only a handful of men.

The problem that the Boer leaders had in keeping together their volunteer army was, to a large degree, an ideological one. For the Boer at the beginning of the war there was nothing more important than his farm and his family. As

Fransjohan Pretorius explains, abstract ideals of nationhood were often not enough to keep him away from the concrete realities of home for too long:

> He was master on his farm and this nationalism was not everything. He had a 'local' nationalism...a parochial nationalism that saw to it that his independence would be kept intact. His own small world must not be destroyed.

That was what Christiaan de Wet had recognized when he had sent his men back to their homes for two weeks. He later wrote that his men had become a 'disorderly crowd of terrified men fleeing before the enemy'. A period at home would enable them to see to their farms and spend time with their families.

Steyn's reply to Kruger was unequivocal. The war must be fought 'to the bitter end'. He had already lost his capital and had seen the British overrun much of the Free State, but he was not about to abandon the struggle 'in a cowardly manner'. He urged Kruger, who after all was the one who had pushed for war in the first place, to stand firm. It was Steyn's telegram combined with the successes of Christiaan de Wet in the Free State that breathed new life into the Boer leadership. Talk of surrender was soon replaced by plans to bring down the great lumbering beast that was the British army.

The new strategy was put into action as Roberts was delayed by De la Rey outside Pretoria. Jan Smuts managed to 'liberate' hundreds of thousands of pounds' worth of gold and coin, and all the reserves of ammunition he could lay his hands on. Trainloads of essential war supplies, guns and

men were spirited out of the city right under Lord Roberts' nose.

Meanwhile, Christiaan de Wet was acting on a message Louis Botha had sent two days earlier. In it he urged De Wet to get behind Roberts and really play havoc with his communications. The very next day the British were ambushed at Heilbron and lost fifty-six food wagons, with 160

The Boers, including Jan Smuts' (seated centre) commando prepared themselves for a guerrilla war.

men taken prisoner. On 7 June the results were even more dramatic. In a triple assault near Roodewal station, De Wet cut the railway line between Pretoria and Kroonstad, took 486 prisoners, wounded 104 and killed thirty-eight. After loading up as much as he could carry, he then put a torch to the mountain of supplies that was waiting to be distributed to Roberts' forces. This destruc-

tion of food, blankets and ammunition worth well over £100,000 was conclusive proof that the Free State spirit was far from broken.

It was not just Christiaan de Wet who was causing trouble. On the last day of May his brother Piet had succeeded in capturing 530 men from one of the most blue-blooded battalions of the Imperial Yeomanry. The unlucky Thirteenth

Battalion contained the Irish Hunt Contingent and the Duke of Cambridge's Own, units that were bulging with earls and viscounts. After riding into the town of Lindley, which unknown to them had been taken back by the Boers, the Thirteenth ducked into some kopjes outside the town and waited to be rescued. Unfortunately, there was no one in the area who could do this, and by the time Lord Methuen arrived on 1 June he discovered that the yeomen had been forced to surrender.

So within a week the De Wet brothers had captured almost 1,000 men and were determined to exploit Roberts' greatest weakness – his reliance on the railway lines. For an army so far away from its supply bases, and scattered across such a vast area, control of the railways was essential. While enabling Roberts to feed, clothe and arm his troops, it simultaneously prevented the Boers from doing the same for theirs. On finding himself without dynamite on one occasion, De Wet wrote:

> It was painful to see the railway line and not be able to do any damage to it. I had made it a rule never to be in the neighbourhood of a railway without interrupting the enemy's means of communication.

By blowing up the railways and cutting the telegraph lines on which the British also depended for their communications, De Wet turned the sheer size of the imperial operation into a distinct disadvantage.

By the beginning of June De Wet had only about 8,000 burghers in the field but, as Roland Schikkerling later wrote, it was a very different body of men from that which had gone home demoralized at the beginning of March:

> It was to some extent a purging and chastening process, which left us only the staunchest and most

steadfast men. The still-beating heart of the Republic, all warm and living, was, by a magical operation, being transplanted in a new body, and a new and determined spirit was asserting itself, principally among those who, at the commencement, were averse to the war. Generally speaking a fuller national consciousness was coming to us.

It was not just the Free State burghers who had undergone a transformation. In a letter dated 28 June, Captain James McKillop of the Yorkshire Imperial Yeomanry described the soldiers waiting for a delivery of winter clothes:

> …the men I speak of are positively in rags all of them having their clothes patched with whatever comes most handy, pieces of sacks, old buck wagon sheeting, leather and sheep skin with hair on. I never thought it possible to see British soldiers in such garbs, [they] are much more like Boers than our own men.

Trooper John Paterson of the Ayrshire Yeomanry was also struck by his appearance:

> Today Hector MacDonald reviewed us all. It was a big difference from the last review I attended at Ayr. No fine uniforms and burnished accoutrements and prancing horses, our old gee-gees could hardly raise a decent gallop to save their lives. We are all out at elbows. I have neighbourless boots on, one has the sole hanging loose. We have nearly all got beards and our helmets are all battered and stained, altogether a disreputable looking crew, it would take our mothers hard work to pick their own sons out.

There was another, more sinister reason why those mothers might have had difficulty in recognizing their sons. From the early days of the war looting had been rife. The Boers looted the empty homes of English colonists in Natal, and the British did the same as Methuen's column made its way northwards through the Cape towards Kimberley. Earl de la Warr, the *Globe* correspondent, wrote:

> It was not too much to say that there was more indiscriminate looting after the Modder River fight in a few days by the British than was done by the Boers in the whole six weeks before the fight.

But a Munster fusilier writing home in December 1899 did not seem to see anything wrong in what he was doing:

> The other day we brought in two pianos, a sofa and two dozen chairs – what you would get £150 for at home – and Billy Jones made short work of them, to boil our dinner with. All the people have left their homes, and we can do as we like with them.

On 11 February 1900, the very first day of Roberts' great march, a farm at Ramdam was looted and set on fire by the advance guides, who left their nickname, 'Tigers', scrawled on the door. The Tigers were none other than Rimington's Guides, to whom the articulate and middle-class L. March Phillipps was proud to belong. Rimington's Tigers became notorious for this kind of activity, and, while distancing himself by his description of the 'slum-bred' Tommy, Phillipps consigns the label 'gentleman's war' even further into the dustbin.

> Looting…is one of his perpetual joys. Not merely looting for profit, though I have seen Tommies take possession of the most ludicrous things – perambulators and sewing machines – but looting for the sheer fun of the destruction; tearing down pictures to kick their boots through them; smashing furniture for the fun of smashing it, and maybe dressing up in women's clothes to finish with, and dancing among the ruins they have made. To pick up a good heavy stone and send it *wallop* right through the works of a piano is a great moment for Tommy.

Pianos were a particular favourite when it came to looting as they made excellent firewood.

This propensity for destruction and looting was increased by the transport disaster at Waterval that occurred just four days into the 480-kilometre march and promptly consigned all the men to half-rations. Looting both subdued the locals and put food in the British army's collectively empty stomach, and although Lord Roberts officially prohibited the activity on his entrance into the Free State, the practice continued unabated.

For the Boers, the violation of their property added a momentum to the nascent 'national consciousness' that Schikkerling had noted, and it hardened the resolve of the men who rejoined De Wet at Sand River.

By 10 June it had become embarrassingly clear to Lord Roberts that the republican armies were not going to surrender despite the fall of their capitals. If that were not bad enough, De Wet seemed to be spearheading some sort of resurgence in what was now called the Orange River Colony. So on 11 June he attempted to crush the only significant force left in the Transvaal by doing battle with Louis Botha.

If De Wet could breathe new life into the burghers of the Free State, then Louis Botha was doing his best to work the same miracle with the Transvaalers. Botha had managed to pull together about 4,000 men against Roberts and his 20,000. The two sides met at Diamond Hill, 30 kilometres east of Pretoria, and fought hard for two days. Roberts' force was too strong and Botha retreated, but it was one of the old-style positive Boer retreats. The casualties were light, and the Boers had managed to thwart Roberts' desire for a decisive result.

There were now two obstacles to a clean finish to the war: Botha and his force in the Transvaal, and De Wet and his force in the Orange River Colony. By the beginning of July, Roberts had decided that he would go after Botha, and that five columns under the appropriately named Sir

Archibald Hunter would track down the elusive De Wet and run him into the ground.

Meanwhile, De Wet was still causing havoc with the railway lines. Lord Roberts issued a proclamation stating that as these attacks could be carried out only with the knowledge of people who lived in the area, anyone living in the vicinity of attacks on communications would henceforth be taken as prisoners of war and have their houses burned down.

There had already been a proclamation on 1 June declaring that as the Colony was now British, anyone found in arms from the fourteenth of that month would be treated as a rebel. What this meant was that their property would be confiscated and their homes would be burned down. It was not a policy that found favour with all of the men who had to enforce it. On 28 June Captain James McKillop wrote:

> I have often had to absolutely wreck a house and leave nothing but a ruin to get what has been wanted, I hate the job most heartily. The scenes I have had with poor women are past description. It is not a nice occupation to render women and little children homeless in this bitterly cold climate and after all their poor miserable shanties are homes, and home is home whether British or Boer – such is war, though the inevitable answer to all is: 'your husband is fighting against us, he should be at home and then his property would be respected.' A soldier should be a hard-hearted man.

Although burning women and children out of their houses seemed a harsh policy to Captain McKillop, Roberts, Kitchener and most of the regular soldiers under them were old hands at it. The euphemistically named 'pacification' of natives had been a standard tactic during the colonial wars, particularly on the north-west frontier in India and in the Sudan.

In the same letter entry Captain McKillop continued:

We wander about like the children of Israel…We are occupied with other columns, in rounding up the brothers de Wet and slim customers they are, playing havoc with the railway and evading every attempt at capture, but it won't go on for ever, they will be caught some day and the war is over.

This was also the view among the higher echelons of the British army as they watched Hunter and his columns gradually closing in for the kill. De Wet, himself a recent victim of farm burning, was now in a town called Bethlehem with President Steyn and an 8,000- strong force. As word reached them of the approach of 20,000 Khakis they made for the Brandwater Basin in the mountain ranges to the south. The Wittebergen and the Roodebergen, or White and Red Mountains, form a horseshoe shape whose end opens on to the Caledon River and the neutral area of Basutoland beyond. The Boers saw the mountains, with only four main passes in or out, as perfect protection from the British. The British saw them as the perfect place in which to trap the Boers. General Hunter and another division from the south-west under Sir Leslie Rundle, or Sir 'Leisurely Trundle' as he came to be known, prepared to block off the passes and bag 8,000 men, a President and a troublemaker.

The problem was that, as these preparations were being made in Bethlehem, the Boers had a change of heart, and on 15 July 2,000 of them, led by De Wet, slipped out through the main pass known as Slabberts Nek. Despite being encumbered with ox-wagons, they were still too fast for the British and they safely made their escape.

The plan that De Wet had made was that he would lead his column out first, two more columns would follow the next day, and the fourth

Initially, farm-burning resulted in women and children being left homeless and exposed on the veld.

column under Marthinus Prinsloo would stay to hold the passes and wait for reinforcements from Natal.

Unfortunately, as soon as De Wet left, morale plummeted, and by 23 July, when Hunter finally began his attack, all three columns were still there.

As the British began to enter the Brandwater Basin and slowly take the passes, the Boers managed to put up a show of force before melting back into the mountains. But there was no doubt that they had been backed into a corner, and after days of low morale, recriminations and arguments about leadership, General Prinsloo finally offered to surrender his men with the condition that they were not treated as prisoners of war. Hunter rejected this condition, but the largest surrender of the war went ahead when he agreed not to confiscate the burghers' property or wagons. After the last-minute escape of 1,500, Hunter had successfully taken about 4,400 Boers out of the game. Most of them spent the rest of the war in a POW camp in Ceylon.

By 14 August 5,000 British soldiers were

chasing or laying in wait for De Wet and his 5-kilometre-long convoy. Knowing that their farms would have been burned down, the burghers simply refused to abandon their covered wagons and De Wet's speed was thus reduced to that of the slowest ox-cart. But thanks to specially trained groups of scouts under Danie Theron and Gideon Scheepers, De Wet managed to outwit and outrun his pursuers.

With the British tight behind him, pushing him north, De Wet was forced to cross the Vaal River and enter the less familiar territory of the Transvaal. Here his men split into three groups. The bulk went into the Transvaal bushveld to recuperate, a small party accompanied President Steyn to see President Kruger in his railway carriage at Malhadadorp and De Wet, with 250 men, decided to return to the Free State always staying one step ahead of the Khakis. Their aim was to return to the Orange River Colony to draw attention away from the departing Steyn.

In order to get back to the Vaal River, De Wet had to cross a range of mountains called the Magaliesbergen. But just as he and his men were approaching a footpath that would lead them to the other side, they discovered from a captured enemy scout that their route was completely blocked by the British. They could not go forwards and they could not go backwards. There was only one thing left to do: they would have to make their own way across the mountains without the benefit of a path.

De Wet's men and their horses were exhausted; they were only able to snatch a quick rest here and there before the scouts would warn them of the approaching British, and they would be on their way again. Part of De Wet's success in evading capture was that, with the judicious use of the *sjambok*, or whip, he could get his whole camp on the move in ten minutes. It was this mixture of fear and respect that persuaded De Wet's men to

The 4,400 Boers taken prisoner in the Brandwater basin were shipped off to Ceylon for the duration of the war.

embark on such a hazardous mountain crossing.

Even a local African said that only baboons had ever crossed the mountains. But to De Wet this was a challenge rather that a discouragement, and his 250 men and their horses began their bold ascent in full view of the British. He later recalled:

It was now so precipitous that there was no possibility of proceeding any further on horseback. The burghers had therefore to lead their horses and had great difficulty even in keeping their own footing. It frequently happened that a burgher fell and slipped backwards under his horse. The climb became now more and more difficult; and when we had nearly reached the top of the mountain, there was a huge slab of granite as slippery as ice, and here man and horse stumbled still more, and were continually falling.

It was a gruelling, terrifying climb made worse by the fear that the British could turn their guns on them at any time because there was absolutely no cover on the rocky mountain face. Although they did not know it, De Wet's men were beyond the range of the big guns, and the British had to look on impotently as the Boers climbed higher and higher.

> We now reached the top of the mountain – entirely exhausted. Through a ravine we had a view that extended for many miles, but wherever we cast our eyes there was no sign of anything that resembled the enemy.

Against all the odds, De Wet had escaped again and so secured for himself the status of a folk hero, not just in South Africa but also in the country whose army was trying so hard to track him down. Arthur Whitlock was a fan:

> De Wet to my mind was a fly-by-night type of figure and, for that reason, young as I was, I admired him, although he was an enemy. He flitted from place to place, causing damage to our troops, then away before we could retaliate.

Little souvenir pictures of De Wet could be bought on the streets of London and songs were composed about his legendary powers of escape. Tales abounded of De Wet having left a town just minutes before the British arrived, and a frustrated cavalry officer was moved to write:

> We have good reason to believe
> Their force is large or small,
> And furnished with some fifty guns
> Or else no guns at all;
> Commanded by one C. de Wet
> Which seems a little queer
> As someone else reported him
> Five hundred miles from here.

The guerrilla campaign waged by De Wet in the Orange River Colony not only convinced many burghers to rejoin their old commandos, but it also had a dispiriting effect on the British troops who thought that the Orange River Colony had been decisively taken. In August, trooper John Paterson wrote:

> The rest of us were ordered to Heilbron to intercept a large commando that was coming in that direction. I can tell you it fairly took us down, we thought we had done with the beggars, but they have a knack of coming up smiling when you least expect them.

As L. March Phillipps remarked, constantly being on the defensive, waiting to be attacked, had a demoralizing effect on the British army:

> Not a gun speaks, not a man is to be seen. We demonstrate before empty hills. Creepily you may conjecture the fierce eyes along the rock edge, but nothing shows. In vain we circle about the plain, advance, retire, curtsey, and set to him; our enemy, like the tortoise, 'will not join the dance'. Nothing is more discouraging. It is like playing to an empty house.

An increasing number of thin columns of smoke across the two republics indicated that farm burning and similar 'pacification' measures were being widely implemented. While De Wet made his

Left: *His mastery of guerilla tactics made Christiaan de Wet a folk hero at home and abroad.*

Overleaf: *Christiaan de Wet was wreaking havoc on the supply and communication lines of the British army. The Khakis seemed powerless to stop him.*

escape through the Magaliesberg mountains, Roberts issued a proclamation, this time relating to the Transvaal:

> It is manifest that the leniency which has been extended to the burghers of the South African Republic is not appreciated by them, but, on the contrary, is being used as a cloak to continue the resistance against the forces of H.M. the Queen.

Buildings harbouring the enemy were to be burned to the ground, burghers not signing the oath of allegiance would be treated as prisoners of war and those breaking the oath would be subject to the death penalty. An Australian, Walker Henderson Thomson of the Bushmen's Corps, wrote to his brother from somewhere near the Magaliesbergen:

> We arrived in Rustenburg after being away 3 months & very much surprised to find that all the farmers that were living on their farms and had passes were out fighting again so we had to burn everything before us. We burnt hundreds of homes [in the] pouring rain & had to turn the women & children out in the wet with only a few clothes & very little food. It is a job that I can't stand & I hope we can get away from it soon. We came over to fight men, not women and children.

And from the Orange River Colony, William Croome wrote:

> Rundle has given orders for all farmhouses to be burnt and we all think it is a beastly shame and don't like the job at all. If old Rundle can't catch de Wet without turning the women and children out on the veldt then it is time he went home and gave up the chase.

The same sentiment was being expressed back in Britain by the Liberal MP David Lloyd George, who told the House of Commons in July 1900:

> A war of annexation against a proud people must be a war of extermination, and that is unfortunately what it seems we are now committing ourselves to – burning homesteads and turning women and children out of their homes.

L. March Phillipps of Rimington's Tigers was still not altogether comfortable with his role in the destruction:

> The various columns that are now marching about the country are carrying on the work of destruction pretty indiscriminately, and we have burnt and destroyed by now many scores of farms. Ruin, with great hardship and want, which may ultimately border on starvation, may be the result to many families…
>
> The worst moment is when you first come to the house. The people thought we had called for refreshments, and one of the women went to get milk. Then we had to tell them that we had come to burn the place down. I simply didn't know where to look.

But the arson continued, and by the end of the war more than 30,000 farms had been burned down.

Biebie van der Merwe's mother as a little girl (far left).

Biebie van der Merwe was told by her grandmother about the time the British came to their farm:

> The house was built of huge sandstone bricks so it could not burn. So they carried all the furniture outside, and one of the pieces was a big grand piano, which was the property of my great-grandmother. It was an heirloom in the family. The commanding officer admired the piano, turned to my great-grandmother and said, 'Madam, may I please play on your piano?' And she, of course, agreed. She probably had no choice. And while he was playing, my grandmother saw the tears run down her mother's face. When the man finished playing he got up and gave the order that the piano must be smashed before they set it on fire. And when he turned around they saw the tears on his cheeks as well.

Farm burning was not an activity restricted to the British. The experience of Marjorie Stuckey's family demonstrates how women were humiliated and the home was violated in the course of this 'gentleman's war':

> The Boers arrived at the farm and demanded breakfast for fifteen. They then said to my grandmother, 'We have had orders to burn your house and your furniture. If you can produce your husband we will not burn the furniture or the house.' So my grandmother said, 'It's quite impossible.' She didn't tell them, but my grandfather was with a flying column hunting down those very Boers. So then they said, 'Well, we will not burn the furniture.' And they helped the family to carry it out. Then they set fire to the house, but they had ransacked every room and they had stolen my grandfather's clothes and my Uncle Clive's clothes and my grandmother's diamond ring and my grandfather's gold watch and chain. And they then set fire to the house and one of them went into Aunt Violet's room and put on her evening cloak and danced around and

said, 'I am Miss Violet Featherstone.' They also opened Uncle Clive's birthday present, which was a book. They wrote comments in it, they drew a picture of Queen Victoria standing behind a horse with 'catch me' written under it. And Mother told of them throwing pieces of iron at the glass doors – the house had lovely French doors – and they were full of glee and excitement, and the family were very upset.

The image of men overcome by excitement as they violated a predominantly female space is one echoed in the letters of Percy Day and seems to have been equally true for both sides:

> We were only there for a few minutes but we did do a little damage in a short time. I put the butt of my rifle through a large looking glass over the mantelpiece and put my foot through a sideboard with glass doors. One of the others smashed up a piano and an organ. The women didn't half scream. I thought they would go for us, but it was an awful sight. I should not have thought that I could have done such a thing, but when you get in with the regular soldiers and have a good gallop we get a bit excited and don't care what comes next.

In addition to farm burning, Kitchener, who had been sent to keep a close eye on the Orange River Colony, sent instructions to his columns that they should 'denude the country of forage and supplies'. His aim was to make it as difficult as possible for the Boer commandos out in the field. This 'scorched-earth' policy was also backed by Lord Roberts. It would restrict the areas in which the commandos could function and might give his men a fighting chance of catching them. When asked to clarify one of his instructions, which included the phrase 'lay waste to...', General Thomas Kelly-Kenny sent the following reply:

> ...gather all food wagons, Cape carts, sheep, oxen,

goats, cows, calves, horses, mares, foals, forage, poultry, destroy what you cannot eat…burn all farmhouses – explain reason (for so doing) as they have harboured enemy and not reported to British authorities as required. Give no receipts, search for hidden stores of ammunition and destroy what you find…The question of how to treat women and children and what amount of food and transport will arise, as regards to the first part they have forfeited all right to consideration and must now suffer for their persistently ignoring warnings against harbouring and assisting our enemy – as regards the second give them the bare amount to reach Winburg and then confiscate all transport. The object is to destroy or remove everything which may help the enemy or his horses or oxen to move. Definition ends.

Captain McKillop, who had

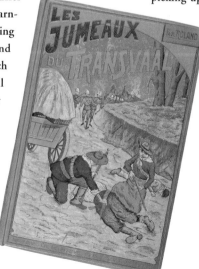

The object of the scorched-earth policy was to deny the Boers on the veld any means of sustenance.

previously expressed his reservations about farm burning, was now more preoccupied with the logistical implications of the policy as livestock was confiscated and crops were destroyed:

I have had a very big job with it all, especially as we are picking up all along the road white and black refugees who are afraid of the Boers who are now becoming very vindictive to all who will not help them. We have also some prisoners. I have all these people to arrange for and see to as

The struggle of the Boers against the British spawned much literature like this French adventure story book written in 1906.

they all have to be carried along somehow. What with the size of the convoy itself and all these additions, I should think I have 500 people, 4,000 oxen and 12,000 sheep all under my charge.

...as our march is one of devastation I turn these great herds of cattle into the standing crops and they soon reduce them to a trampled worthless mess which is our object this march – the purpose of destroying all the possible sources of food for the Boers which I think will be the only way to get at them.

As for Kelly-Kenny's instruction to explain the reason why the farm was about to be burned down, L. March Phillipps and the Tigers seemed to need no such justification:

I do not gather that any special reason or cause is alleged or proved against the farms burnt...Anyway we find that one reason or other generally covers pretty nearly every farm we come to, and so to save trouble we burn the lot without inquiry.

Lieutenant Jack Wynn sent a letter and photographs home to his mother describing exactly how farms were being destroyed:

May 16th 1901

My dear Mother,

...We did some good as we captured a good many prisoners and burnt every farm and all forage and mealies we could not use ourselves. I was in my element as I had my share of farms: what they do is, the Captains of the company get four farms told off to his company and a section goes to each. When I go to one I put my lookout men out as we often get sniped at, and then get my horses under cover and start first by searching the house for rifles and ammunition; then search the outbuildings for mealies and forage and fill all the section's nose-bags with mealies and tie a bundle or two of forage on our saddles, and then burn all the remainder.

Catch all the cluckings. I am A1 at catching cluckings now. The men kill all the pigs, and have them cut up in no time. Each man has a piece, either a leg or piece of the rib as far as it will go round. I killed 20 at one farm. Next I drive in all the horses I can find on the Veldt into what they call a Cattle Krawl [sic] and take all that are fit to ride and loose all that are too young, and drive all the sheep and cattle back with me; sometimes we find from 500 to 1,000 head of stock on a farm. If the man that owns that farm has surrendered and is in one of our refugee Laargers [sic], I give a receipt to his wife. If he is on commando still, they get no receipt. I found in one farm 10 Mauser rifles and 1,000 (about) rounds of ammunition under the floor in one of the rooms. I go into all the rooms and turn everything upside down, cut the mattresses of the beds open to look for rifles, you would not like that I know...

I myself if I am sent to a farm to see what is in it and to get the women out I never hesitate to burn the place before I leave, and only give the people five minutes to pack up and get into the wagon. I have no pity on them no matter how they weep, they are far worse than the men.

Lieutenant Jack Wynn in a photograph he sent home to his mother.

It is not clear what Lieutenant Wynn meant when he said that Boer women were 'far worse than the men', but it was certainly true that their feelings about the justness of their cause and the necessity of war were as strong as and often stronger than those of their men. Back in November 1899 John Moody Lane had remarked:

> The women are certainly keeping the men up to war fever. I think it would be a darned good thing to put 'breeches' on some of them and send them to the front.

There was talk of an Amazonian corps of women going off to fight and rumours of women dressing as men to go out on commando, but most were concerned with keeping the farms going until their men returned. With women taking on a new role as head of the household, the old patriarchal order had to be suspended – especially, as Rose van Rensburg makes clear, if the women were to retain their dignity in the face of the depredations of British soldiers:

> The women were very rebellious after their menfolk had left, and they had to remain behind with the children. So they were very bitter against the English [sic], because they were treated very roughly and the English did not treat them as they ought to.

These women, or *vrouws*, also had to deal with Africans working on their farms who would not show the same deference to a white woman as they would to a white man. Being humiliated by both the Britisher and the black man bred an even stronger determination to win this war. The independence of the republics and all that it entailed for the hierarchy of races was a subject close to the *vrouw's* heart.

So, after Cronje's surrender at Paardeberg, when the Boers started to return home demoral-

Although women were rarely combatants they were certainly at the front line of hostilities during the guerrilla phase of the war.

ized, it was more often than not their wives who persuaded them to go back out into the field with the parting shot: 'I can get another husband but I can't get another Free State.' Far from subduing the women's spirit, farm burning and the destruction of their property only increased the sense of a common struggle among the women who were forced to huddle together, homeless, on the veld. This is what L. March Phillipps noticed as the Tigers vigorously carried out Roberts' scorched-earth policy:

It is curious coming to household after household and finding the whole lot of them, women and children, so unanimous, so agreed in the spirit in which they face their afflictions. It is not often these days that you see one big, simple, primitive instinct, like love of country, acting on a whole people at once.

The Boer Roland Schikkerling wrote, somewhat elegiacally, in his book *Commando Courageous*:

The female bootmaker, cattle-driver and farmer is a by-product of this war. She is a fighter, grim and lone, not on the so-called glorious field of combat but in the quiet cornfield and the pastures; not in the smoke of battle, but in her wrecked and burnt-down home. She is a by-product which by some subtle alchemy outshines the primary product…as gold is retorted from baser metals and refined by an ordeal of fire.

Throughout the war, women gave the commandos much more than just psychological support. Ada Prinsloo's mother, along with women whose husbands were in the field, had a narrow escape:

Altogether there were twelve women. They were providing food for a Boer commando. They thought the Boer commando was coming and when they looked again, much later in the evening, they saw it was an English commando…it was the Khakis, not the Boers.

They fled with what they could take with them and they fled into a cave. They had just been baking dough to make griddle cakes. My mother tied some of this dough in a roll around her body.

The experience of hiding in caves to escape the British was not an uncommon one. While Phole Mokoena's father was away working as an *agterryer* for his boss, his mother looked after the boss's wife:

My mother and the white woman were staying in the cave. She smeared this woman with what you call it, it was almost like dye or paint so that she should look like a black woman. So that she could take food and then come back and stay with my mother in the cave. There were a group of them, she was not alone. My mother stayed with these white women because she respected them. She stayed with them and cooked for them, she did everything for them in the mountains.

As well as food, women also provided the commandos with vital intelligence. Manie Maritz, whose father was a famous Boer general, recognized the importance of women to the burghers in the field:

A woman was not a soldier, but she was a spy. My father's sisters carried reports from one group to the other, they could move around. I think a woman had as much to do with the war as the men did.

This perhaps explains Captain McKillop's reaction when he came across a sizable laager of women who were living huddled together on the veld near Mafeking:

The women were not a bad-looking lot and some of the children were nice looking had both been clean, but I had no sympathy for them at all as their menfolk were out fighting and every one of them had taken the oath of allegiance and had passes given to them, and their goods had been unmolested by former columns passing through the country, and here they were fighting away as hard as ever. I don't know what will be the end of it all, the Boers seem to be a different kind of animal. I don't believe that any other white race would do this, they have [not] a spark of honour amongst them, high or low.

As the guerrilla war spread, engulfing more and more of the population, women were not the only non-combatants to be sucked into the conflict. Africans were recognized by both sides as a source of labour and as providers of food. Each side believed that if the Africans were not supporting them, then they were supporting the enemy.

Willem Pietersen's birth certificate shows that he was born in 1881, but the memory of what happened to his black father a hundred years ago is still vivid:

It was on a Thursday afternoon when the English shot my dad. My dad was walking down to the fields. When he reached the cattle which were in the fields, the British asked: Why are the cattle in the field? It is because you are helping the Boers. Because of that they shot my father dead. Dead.

As a young African boy growing up in the Orange River Colony, Jacob Motawey and the people around him did not really understand what was happening when the British swept through on their horses:

We thought the soldiers were playing but they were actually soldiers of war. They were drilling and marching and we thought they were dancing, we thought they were playing but in actual fact it was war...Their horses made dust and whenever we saw the troops coming we would run. People were afraid. The troops meant war every time we saw them. They said they were looking for rebels and we ran as they approached.

But Dorah Ramothibe, also in the Orange River Colony, knew from harsh experience that she should feel more threatened by the Boer rebels than by their pursuers:

The Boers were rascals. We were scared of them. We hid from them, because if they found us, they would burn our houses down with us in them and we would die. There were people who were burnt in their houses.

The situation was not much different in the Transvaal. When Anna Molakeng saw mounted Boers approaching she knew that there would be trouble. Her father told her that they had come for food and men:

They were looking for horses and cows. They found the cows and they would eat half and just leave the rest when they were full. When the white man saw our black men on the field, they would capture them with their guns. We as women would be left behind and would be surprised as to what was happening. We would run away to the fields and we would take our belongings and hide in the fields and the bushes. Everybody would hide and we would remain in hiding. There were no men there, no boys. They had all been captured by the Boers.

As well as the Africans caught in the middle, and the *agterryers* who had often been given little choice in following their *baas* on commando, there were many black people who, for various reasons, actively involved themselves in the war. One of the reasons was money. The devastation of the country and the high rates of unemployment meant that in some areas working for the British army was the only job a man could get. Gideon Malalose's father Jeponiah was born and brought up on a Boer farm in the north-eastern Transvaal, but he joined the

Any blacks caught working as scouts for the British would be shot on sight.

British as a scout in an undeniably pragmatic spirit:

> The point was that in that town there were more English than Boers…Secondly, the Boers didn't have the money to pay them, and the English had the money to pay them and were also suppliers of food and all the rest of it. They were treated like soldiers even though they were not soldiers. So the natural thing to do was to join the Victoria side. Join the English, you get paid, you get uniformed and you are safer that way. The English won all the battles, so who would join the loser? Simple as that.

After decades of being treated like a slave by the Boers, fighting for the British also gave Jeponiah Malalose the opportunity to redefine the power balance:

> You were somebody because you had a gun in your hand. You had a horse which you could ride and you commanded respect, not only amongst your own people, but, let's face it, when [my father] approached the Boers…sometimes the Boers had to run away for their lives and that added to his self-importance.

That feeling can only have been increased by being given the opportunity to legitimately destroy the very thing that the Boer held so dear – his homestead:

> My father did in fact join parties that burned houses and they robbed farms. That's why it was a lucrative business to join and forage in these farmhouses and set them all on fire and all that. It was part of the game, as it were…the idea was to avoid these Boers having a place where to hide, that was the main thing. It was part of the war strategy. But I don't think my father ever thought of the strategy being justified or not justified. To him it was just getting orders, as simple as that.

The war in South Africa was being fought in an atmosphere where looting, burning and devastation were regarded as acceptable weapons with which to defeat the enemy. While being impossible to quantify, behaviour that overstepped even these marks was almost inevitable. Gideon Malalose is under no illusions about what happened on some of the farm-burning expeditions in which his father took part:

> They would sexually assault these Boer girls. The point was this, it's not easy to always find a white woman around anywhere. Where he grew up on the farm, a woman was a white one, sacrosanct. Here was a situation where you can take these girls and they can't refuse, they can't defend themselves, and very often things like that did in fact take place. My father generalized on things like that, but I don't think that he was holier than thou. The other soldiers did that and I don't think he could have refrained from that also.

Although Lord Roberts issued an order

prohibiting the arming of black scouts, conditions in the field made it increasingly untenable for the local commanders to send the scouts out undefended.

Gideon Malalose's father was certainly aware of the penalty for being caught working for, or even suspected of working for, the British:

> If it had been discovered that they were spies they would have been shot without fail, and they knew that if they're ever found with a uniform, with the Khakis, even if they were found elsewhere, they would be shot on sight.

A letter written by Captain James McKillop, who was dealing with guerrilla units in the western Transvaal, illustrates how some Boers viewed black participation on the British side:

> We have a rag tag and bobtail mob down here against us who are up to all kinds of villainy. A few days ago they murdered two telegraphists and two blacks who went to mend the wire…the whites were riddled with bullets which had been fired at close quarters as to singe their clothes, the blacks they had first shot then pounded to a jelly with their rifle butts.

Rina Viljoen's father, who had fought at the Battle of Magersfontein and had tried to rescue Cronje at Paardeberg, was now fighting the guerrilla war.

The justification given for his actions against the blacks typified Boer thinking at that time:

> When they encountered a group of English soldiers they would attack them. As soon as they felt overpowered they would flee. It's what they called attack and run. And then one day they encountered an English soldier with two blacks. And they were spies. Usually the blacks, who knew the territory well, would accompany the English soldiers through those areas to look for the groups of guerrillas. The two groups spotted each other. At that stage my father and most of the Boers were wearing old English uniforms, because they had no other clothes to wear and nobody supplied them with any supplies. When they came near enough they shot the two blacks but they did not kill the English soldier. They just took his clothes. They argued that the blacks should not help the English. It was not their war.

The wearing of British uniforms by the Boers was understandable but against all the conventions of 'civilized' warfare. Completely sealed off from the outside world and increasingly denied access to support from the farmhouses, khaki uniforms were often the only clothes available to the guerrillas. When any British were captured, they would be told to undress and tattered rags would be swapped for a slightly less tattered uniform. The problem, as Rina Viljoen's story demonstrates, is that wearing a uniform could enable the Boers to get dangerously close to the British before being recognized as the enemy. After a number of reported abuses, it was proclaimed that any Boer found in a British uniform would be shot on sight.

This difficulty of distinguishing friend from foe exemplifies one of the distinctive features of the war. The traditional order of things was disrupted as unlikely allegiances were forged and the bonds of friendship and sometimes even family were torn apart. Dr Kay de Villiers goes some way to explaining:

> I think it's a war of greater complexity than we ever thought. It was simple when I was boy, it was Boer against Brit. [But] it was also a civil war in the sense that people from the Cape province and the town who were British subjects found themselves bound by loyalty or blood or politically, or whatever, to take sides with the two republics.

The situation in the Cape was only one of

The arming of black scouts was inevitable and necessary although it had been officially prohibited by Lord Roberts.

Clothing became so scarce that when the Boers captured British soldiers they often captured their trousers as well.

have to face – our own kith and kin; but the devils deserve nothing less than they got – shot.

One of the most resonant splits was between Christiaan de Wet and his brother Piet. Back in July of 1900, despite a number of successful guerrilla strikes, Piet de Wet decided that the Boers could never win the war and turned himself over to the British. In 1901 Piet sent a message to his brother, explaining his own actions and strongly urging Christiaan to give up the fight as well:

Which is better for the republics – to continue the struggle and run the risk of total ruin as a nation or to submit? Could we for a moment think of taking back the country if it were offered to us, with thousands of people to be supported by a government that has not a farthing…even if we received help from Europe? Put passionate feeling aside for a moment and use common sense, and you will then agree with me that the best thing for the people and the country is to give in, be loyal to the new government, and try to get responsible government.

The messenger was flogged and sent back with the promise that if Christiaan de Wet ever came across his traitorous brother he would shoot him down like a dog. The 'joiner', the Boer who fought for the British, would soon become a hate-figure in Afrikaner legend. Ada Prinsloo, whose father was on commando, summed up how many Boers felt then and still feel now:

My father was not nearly as opposed to the English as he was to the joiners. He could, plain and simply, not stand the joiners. It felt to him that what they had done was just too unforgivable. To betray your nation and your country, to betray your everything! They carried that grudge for a long time after the war. I know that because I was already a girl and slightly older when Daddy said, 'The English came

numerous examples showing a community divided by conflicting interests. It was not just a white dilemma. The Barolongs, the Basothos and the Bakgatlas all had men on both the British and the Boer sides. Even the Khakis found themselves fighting against fellow Britons who had joined the Boer side. Sergeant George Wallace wrote to a friend:

The Boer Army is full of all nationalities. Two Boers were brought in here the other day. One was named MacDonald – a thorough Scotchman – and the other Edwards – an Englishman. So you can tell what we

because they had to. They were commanded to come here the same way as we were commanded to fight for our country. In the same way they came here to protect their country. But the joiners, they stabbed us in the back.'

While Roberts was evolving farm burning into a full scorched-earth policy, Redvers Buller was slowly but surely working his way northwards through Natal and into the south-east Transvaal. He had not allowed farm burning to be carried out by his army, and this was not just because they were on British territory. In Buller's opinion, suc-

cess or failure against the Boers would be achieved only in the field. Unless the British could hold the ground in between the towns, collecting Boer capitals was mere trophy-waving and would not result in a decisive victory.

Instructed by Roberts to remain on the defensive after the relief of Ladysmith, Buller achieved some significant successes as his army moved north, most notably outflanking 7,000 Boers in the Biggarsberg range in May 1900, and then ejecting another 4,500 from the hills around Laings Nek in June. By August, Bobs was ready to turn his attention back to his eastern offensive and arranged that the two armies should make a joint attack on Louis Botha in the Transvaal.

After methodically working their way up the Transvaal, opening railway lines and holding ground as they went, Buller's forces arrived south

Kruger's flight to France and the annexation of the Transvaal prompted Lord Roberts to believe, erroneously, that the war was practically over.

of Belfast, where they linked up with Roberts and formulated a plan for a combined assault.

Louis Botha and about 7,000 of his men were dug in around the Pretoria–Delagoa Bay railway line. The key to his position was a kopje which jutted out from the 32-kilometre-long Boer front.

Botha, too, had realized the significance of the kopje and had posted sixty of his best men from the Johannesburg police, to hold it at all costs. After withstanding a three-hour bombardment by forty British guns, these men still managed to put up a stout defence when the infantry came over the top. Their tenacity was remarkable, but their position was hopeless and eventually they were overcome. As soon as the kopje had fallen to the British, the Boer lines seemed to cave in and Buller's army could celebrate a victory in what was the last significant set-piece battle of the war, the battle of Dalmarutha. The British pursuit proved typically ineffective, but just three days later Buller could content himself with securing the release of all 2,000 British prisoners of war who had been held at Nooitgedacht.

After several weeks of chasing Botha and his much-reduced forces around the Transvaal, Buller returned to England. The public had certainly forgiven him for the disasters of Black Week and Spion Kop, but it seemed that the establishment had not. He received no military honours and was bundled back to Aldershot to resume his old job of training the army corps.

Buller was not the only man to leave South Africa in October. Paul Kruger, who had escaped to Mozambique in September, left for France on a ship provided for him by the Queen of Holland. It was to be the last he would see of his promised land.

Christiaan de Wet never came to terms with the fact that his brother Piet turned from a Republican hero to a 'joiner' who eventually fought against the Boers.

Although the British lion had captured both of the Boer capitals, the burghers were far from beaten.

With Kruger gone, the Boer republics annexed (Roberts proclaimed the annexation of the Transvaal on 25 October), and Botha's forces fragmented, Lord Roberts felt it safe to declare at the beginning of December that war was 'practically over'. A few more months would ensure that the scorched-earth policy had pacified any Boer supporters and starved the guerrillas into submission.

After seeing Kitchener set in place as the new Commander-in-Chief in South Africa, and ousting Lord Wolseley as Commander-in-Chief back in Britain, Roberts returned to a hero's welcome and, unlike Buller, an earldom and £100,000.

*The blockhouse system would prove instrumental in
finally removing from the Boers their greatest
advantage – mobility.*

CHAPTER SIX

The Bitter End

The proper strategy consists in inflicting as telling blows as possible on the enemy's army, and then in causing the inhabitants so much suffering that they must long for peace, and force the government to demand it. The people must be left with nothing but their eyes to weep with over the war.

ADVICE FROM GENERAL SHERIDAN TO BISMARCK, QUOTED APPROVINGLY
IN A LETTER TO *THE TIMES* OF 25 OCTOBER 1901

I don't know how many funerals there were a day. Someone said that if you put all the mothers' tears together, you'd have enough to fill a dam. I can remember them saying that.

ROSE BRIERS ON THE CONCENTRATION CAMPS

It wasn't just the Boers who believed that God was on their side. In this photograph soldiers of the British Army can be seen at a church parade in front of a hospital in Graaff Reinet.

LORD ROBERTS' ASSESSMENT OF the situation in South Africa had been a triumph of optimism over realistic observation. The Boer forces in the Transvaal had now joined the Orange River Colony in full-scale guerrilla warfare, and the British army was on the defensive. The policy of burning homes and farms, as well as inciting many men to rejoin their commandos, also meant that the primary reason for deserting the commando – returning to the farm – had been removed. By the end of the year there were almost as many burghers back in arms as there had been at the beginning of the war.

In October the Boer leaders had held another council of war to discuss how best to counter the scorched-earth policy. An escalation of the guerrilla war would inevitably result in women and children being dragged even further into the conflict, but there seemed little alternative. The council resolved that the guerrilla war would continue and that they would also invade Cape Colony and Natal. Not only were there thousands of Afrikaners who might rise up in rebellion, but it seemed highly unlikely to the Boers that the British would implement the scorched-earth policy on their own territory.

While the Boers put their trust in God, Trooper John Paterson mused on the irony of his situation:

I wish you saw us at church here…We sit with our rifles over our knees to keep the wind from blowing away our Bibles as it were. Sometimes our horses are standing behind, saddled and bridled and half an hour after the benediction we are doing our best to kill brother Boer…I don't see what the poor devils are fighting for, they are simply ruining their country.

The guerrilla attacks on trains and the blowing up of bridges continued. In the Orange River Colony, Christiaan de Wet suffered a major setback in November when he was out-Boered at Bothaville. The British attacked while his men were sleeping, and he lost 131 of the rearguard along with all of his artillery. The Boer losses would have been much greater had the main British column been quicker in arriving on the scene, but it was an important psychological boost to the Khakis nevertheless. The Transvaal burgher Roland Schikkerling noticed that the British were changing their tactics:

> The enemy is adopting our methods of fighting. At one time it was said an Englishman is like a chicken. He retires at sunset, and nothing need be feared from him after dark. Now, however, he is making night raids all over the country, and practising our own stratagems upon us.

The tables were soon turned, though, when in December Koos de la Rey attacked a convoy in the Transvaal and bagged 1,800 oxen and the contents of over a hundred supply wagons. Within a fortnight he and General Beyers had also taken General Clements completely by surprise at Nooitgedacht. They managed to inflict almost 650 casualties before looting his camp.

With the scorched-earth policy taking hold, and with no means of getting fresh supplies into the country, the Boers were dependent on the success of raids like these for their very survival. Ammunition, in particular, had been in

General Koos de la Rey inflicted 650 casualties and bagged 1,800 oxen and a hundred supply wagons.

short supply since Black Week. As the number of Mauser bullets dwindled and the weapons themselves needed replacing, the Boers were forced to use the Lee Metford rifles taken from the British. Louis Hefer, who was in the Bloemfontein Artillery, told his son about one of the more resourceful methods of procuring ammunition:

> They would go to the spot where the Khakis had slept the previous night. The foot soldiers would throw away their excess cartridges and they would pick them up, and he said that when the afternoon came they would shoot the hell out of the English with their own cartridges.

Kitchener had been in his new position as Commander-in-Chief for less than three weeks when Free State Boers led by General Kritzinger and Judge Hertzog invaded Cape Colony. They, and 2,000 of their men, had crossed the Orange River on 16 December 1900, narrowly failing to take De Wet with them.

So the guerrilla war had escalated, the Boers were rallying to the call, and Cape Colony had been invaded. It was not the most auspicious of starts to what was supposed to be a mopping-up operation by Kitchener. Neither had it been particularly helpful of Lord Roberts to have thrown such a positive light on the position in South Africa, that the War Office back in Britain was starting to pull troops out.

What Kitchener realized in December was that the war was not 'practically over'; it had simply moved into another phase. It was now all-out guerrilla warfare, and for as long as Boer families remained on the veld the guerrillas would have some means of sustenance. The great guerrilla tactician Mao Tse-tung would write, years later, that a guerrilla moves through the people like a fish moves through water. Kitchener took the decision in 1900 to remove that water.

The practice of massing Boer families together in large camps had already been established by Lord Roberts when he was Commander-in-Chief. After the occupation of Johannesburg and Pretoria, there were many Boer families left behind who then became dependent on the British for food and clothing. So irritated was Lord Roberts by persistent guerrilla attacks on the railway line bringing supplies that, in July 1900, he sent several hundred families back to Louis Botha by open railway truck, saying that it was his responsibility to look after his own people. But this was more a gesture of frustration and a means of applying pressure to the Boers than a well-thought-out policy, and it did not resolve the question of what to do with the increasingly large number of people

made homeless by his scorched-earth initiative.

Roberts' policy of allowing surrendered Boers to return to their farms was proving counterproductive, as there was nothing to stop them from taking up arms again as soon as a Boer commando arrived in the area. It was, therefore, suggested by one of Roberts' generals that the 'hands-uppers' – men who had surrendered – and their families

Concentration camps like this one at Norvals Point were soon dotted across the former Boer Republics.

should instead be concentrated in a place where they could be both protected from the pressure to break the oath of allegiance and kept an eye on. Three camps were duly set up in the Orange River Colony and the Transvaal.

The 'concentration camps', as they later came to be called, had notoriously been used by the Spanish General, Valeriano Weyler, during the Cuban insurrection against Spain in 1896–7. Somewhere in the region of 200,000 people had died in his camps, and his methods had received

widespread condemnation. Undeterred, Kitchener decided on the full-scale implementation of the camp policy, as his army memorandum of 21 December 1900 makes clear:

> The General Officer Commanding-in-Chief is desirous that all possible means be taken to stop the present guerrilla warfare. Of the various measures suggested for the accomplishment of this object, one that has been strongly recommended, and has lately been successfully tried on a small scale, is the removal of all men, women and children and natives from the districts which the enemy persistently occupy. This course has been pointed out by surrendered Burgers who are anxious to finish the war, as the most effective method of limiting the endurance of the Guerrillas, as the men and women left on the farms, if disloyal, willingly supply burgers, if loyal dare not refuse to do so.

The memorandum goes on to describe how the families brought in from the veld should be placed near the railway line to make it easier to feed them. They should also be split into two categories and treated accordingly: firstly, those who were strictly speaking refugees – the families of hands-uppers or non-combatants; and secondly the families of men who were still on commando.

Kitchener's instructions were thoroughly implemented. By the end of the war there would be forty-six camps in all. Appalling death rates in the concentration camps would bring accusations of a deliberate British policy of genocide. For Marie Proudfoot, whose mother was interned at a

Lord Kitchener of Khartoum was behind the full-scale implementation of the concentration camp system.

camp outside Mafeking, there is still no doubt in her mind as to where the blame lay:

> Initially it was not so bad, but when Kitchener took over, things were over and done with. He was a murderer. Initially they left the women and children on the farms but when he took over it was goodbye. Then everybody had to go. He did not care what he said or what he did. How much blood of the innocent flowed here? Innocent children in those cemeteries.

Military men such as Major John Buist take a more pragmatic view:

> I think that the circumstances being what they were at the time, that the only way you could combat the guerrilla warfare was to have something of that sort, concentration camps, where the families of the people in the field were separated so they couldn't refuel, as you might say.

The question is still being debated a hundred years later: even if the camps were militarily necessary to bring the war to an end, was the culpable negligence, resulting in suffering and death on such a scale, distinguishable from a deliberate policy of extermination? Janice Farquharson, whose family were besieged at Kimberley, thinks it is:

> This is part of the tragedy, the appalling tragedy that the war was. That if you're going to have a total war, everybody's going to suffer, and this is what was happening here. And as far as the concentration camps were concerned, I think what this was was inefficiency. It was not as some extremists would claim a policy of genocide.

Millions of sheep, cattle and poultry were slaughtered as part of the scorched-earth policy.

Lord Kitchener was a man in a hurry, and this was all too clearly demonstrated in his organization of the camps. He knew that the sooner he could clear up the mess in South Africa, the sooner he could fulfil a long-held ambition of becoming Commander-in-Chief in India. Perhaps this is what blinded him to the inevitable consequences of cramming together thousands of people in a small space with inadequate medical care, sanitation and nutrition. Dr Kay de Villiers sees the camps as an extreme expression of British impotence in the face of the new kind of war being waged by the Boers:

> I think one must look upon the camps, and I'm not going to try to justify anything one way or the other, as a manifestation of the frustration felt by the British High Command. The war would not come to an end, they had no answer for guerrilla warfare. None of the things they knew worked. They were not making any headway.

Entire families and their servants were swept off the veld, loaded into trucks and taken to the nearest camp. Captain James McKillop observed in his diary:

> The refugees are a most amusing sight – they have to be packed like herrings on the wagons. I saw 25 women and children in one wagon and the others are nearly as crowded.

Marie Proudfoot's mother was one of those forced into crowded wagons by natives, after seeing her farm destroyed and her home burned:

> They loaded them on to an ox wagon – the blacks – and took them away. The whole wagon was overloaded. They did not even have time to gather some clothes to take with them. Nothing. Before they left the farm they killed the sheep, the chickens were killed. The wheat was taken and thrown out and the house was set alight. The English, the Khakis did that. The chickens were caught and tied to the horses' saddles. They hung there like sausages. They destroyed everything.

This depiction of Boer women being taken to a camp, although inaccurate in its detail, demonstrated how the actions of the British were being seen abroad.

In their eyes, one of the greatest indignities suffered by the Boer families as they were removed from their homes was that their removal was partially effected by Africans helping the British to clear the veld. Centuries of black subjugation by whites was reversed at a stroke, as women like Rose van Rensburg's mother found themselves humiliated:

It was a very cold morning when they arrived in Bethulie. That morning the frost lay white, and the little children were cold and hungry and everything, and there they had to disembark...And, my mother told me, as they disembarked with their few belongings, the coloureds were there – Hottentots, my mother called them. She said they now had the upper hand and were just plain cheeky to us, and had no

compassion for us, and chased us along until we finally reached the camp.

Each camp was allocated one superintendent, one doctor and a few nurses. Shelter was provided by bell tents, which, as Dr Kay de Villiers indicates, were often far too old to give any real protection from the extreme changes in temperature:

When these camps were established they were over-crowded. Large numbers of people came in; they had to find a place and they were hungry, they were tired, they were cold. This is one of the strange things about the South African climate. A winter's day is one of the most beautiful days that you can have, it's warmer than the English summer's day, but the night is a frosty, bitterly cold experience. And this is where they had to find shelter in a tent, or in tents. Crowded together.

Food rations were minimal, and fresh fruit and vegetables almost unheard of. It was not that the British army was ignorant about healthcare. Victorian society had seen huge advances in medical understanding – germ theory had been widely accepted since the 1850s, and the latest developments in antiseptic surgery were already thirty years old. But, as was shown during the typhoid epidemic at Bloemfontein, the Royal Army Medical Corps was not sufficiently well organized to keep its own men healthy, let alone the population of the Transvaal and the Orange River Colony. As Dr Kay de Villiers makes clear, there were particular reasons why the Boers were more susceptible to certain diseases than the British forces:

I think in understanding the medical status of the two Boer republics, one must in the first instance under-stand and acknowledge that they were two isolated communities. They had no contact with the seaport.

They have lived in isolation now for virtually a hundred years…and when they are exposed suddenly to a large influx of people from outside, they come into contact with the organisms that carry disease, particularly measles. The Boer population was an unexposed one, and when the children were in the camps, close together, overcrowded, that is the way the virus spread.

The most common causes of death in the camps were measles, pneumonia and dysentery, and the most vulnerable of the internees were young children. As Rose Briers remembers, conditions in the tents did nothing to alleviate their suffering:

> I know they treated the little children very badly in the camp. That I remember. They had to live in tents.

Mrs de Kock used to say that at night it was so wet because of the rain that she would make a little place for her children up on the table. Many of them died.

Living in isolated communities meant that Boer families were used to treating illnesses themselves. Boer doctors did not have access to modern medical training, and their expertise was still rooted in seventeenth-century traditions. This was not true, of course, for the urbanized Afrikaners, but the vast majority of people in the concentration camps were from rural Boer families. The culture of hospitalization was completely alien to them and, as Rina Viljoen makes clear, mothers in the camps dreaded their children being taken from them:

> There were a lot of diseases in the camp. People were often sick and many died, especially the children…and when the authorities learnt there was a sick child in your tent, they took that child to a hospital. And the Boer women strongly believed that within three days that child would be dead. You were also not allowed to visit that child in the hospital. So if a child became ill you just hid him in the tent and kept him there.

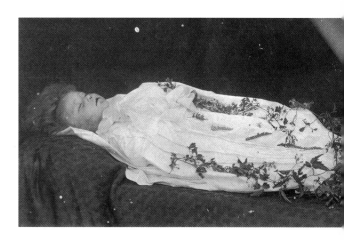

A clash of medical cultures did nothing to alleviate the death rate among children in the concentration camps.

A culture of mistrust developed between the camp medical staff and the Boer women. The doctors and nurses could not understand why mothers would deliberately frustrate their attempts to give 'proper' medical attention to the children, and the mothers saw the removal of their children, usually closely followed by their death, as another method of punishment. Biebie van der Merwe's grandmother had been taken to a concentration camp in the eastern Transvaal:

> Her small brother became ill. The child was sick when they were taken to the concentration camp…And her mother was in deadly fear that the English doctor might treat the child. They were afraid to let the children go to a hospital, and therefore they had to take this child outside and play with him…One day he was so ill, so feverish that he could not walk. And they held him up on both sides. The brother and sister held his hands, and they walked with him between the tents – One…two …three…Up in the air!…Just so that the doctor should not see the child…He was almost unconscious and could not walk…they were afraid of the medicine.

Ann Raats' grandmother, Anna Griesel, was thirty-one when war broke out. Her husband went on commando, leaving her to look after five young children. Eventually Anna and her children were taken to a concentration camp. Her youngest child, Nellie, contracted dysentery and died:

> My grandmother was very sad at the loss of this little girl, and the thing that worried her most was that there were no coffins in which to bury the dead. They had to be wrapped in a blanket and laid in the ground. At this time a British captain came riding over to see whether there was anything he could do to assist her.

Despairing mothers would often try to disguise the sickness of their child to prevent them being removed from their care.

The severe shortage of nurses in the white concentration camps meant that they were desperately overworked. The black camps were not allocated nurses at all.

> He also wanted to commiserate with her over the death of this little girl. My grandmother explained the difficulty of burying her without a coffin, and he said he would see what he could do. In due course a couple of soldiers brought her a munitions box which was just the right size for a coffin for a four-year-old child. My grandmother wrapped her little girl in her second petticoat, laid her in the munitions box and she was buried.

This tragedy had a surprising postscript. After the war ended Anna Griesel's Boer husband did not return and was presumed killed in action. The British captain married Anna, and Ann Raats' mother was their first child. It was another example of the difficulty of a situation in which ties of family, kinship and race were often set against each other.

This manifested itself in the camps as it had done on the veld. Marie Proudfoot still feels particularly bitter towards the Boers who worked for the British and taunted the internees:

The Joiners treated those women in the camps much worse than the English speakers did. They thought they were just 'It'. They ridiculed them. 'Your husbands are fighting and you are dying of hunger and we are getting enough food!' They got everything they wanted.

Dr Kay de Villiers sees this an inherent problem in the camp administration:

Many of the camps were run by renegade Boers, by hands-uppers who defected to the other side. People who have guilt feelings against those whom they feel they've betrayed or have been told that they have betrayed, whether they believe it or not. And you get the small, miserable interaction between people who are too close together and have no love. And I think this is what happened and this is why in South Africa in that war, one had the elements of a civil war.

Pieter Colyn, whose father, Lemuel, had acted as a spy for the British, would feel the burden of history as a small child registering at school:

When I said my name the teacher said I must get up. He said, 'If your name is Pieter Colyn you must stand up and turn around so that the whole class can see what the child of a traitor looks like.'

Emily Hobhouse became the Boers' champion when she railed against the conditions in the white camps.

As Kitchener turned the military screw, he also explored the possibility of a political solution. The Boer leadership had, hitherto, been opposed to any talk of a peace settlement, and had even accused the intermediaries sent by the British of being traitors. But in February 1901 Kitchener decided to send the wife of Louis Botha back to her husband with a message that he was prepared to discuss a negotiated peace settlement. The only thing that would not be open to discussion was the British annexation of the former republics.

On 28 February Kitchener and Botha met for a conference at Middelburg, where Kitchener took a conciliatory tone. The two men parted with Kitchener agreeing to forward a set of proposals to the British government. The proposals included a general amnesty for both Boers and rebels; compensation for war damage and a £1 million payment of Boer debts; the swift return of all prisoners of war; self-government at the earliest opportunity; and an understanding that any political rights accorded to non-whites would not be given until the whites had been granted representative government.

The proposals as put forward by Kitchener underwent significant revision as they passed through the hands of the British High Commissioner Sir Alfred Milner and the Cabinet. By the time the formal offer had been sent back to Botha for his approval, the concessions had been considerably toned down, and the clause giving amnesty to the rebels had been completely excised. On the matter of the black franchise, Chamberlain declared that an agreement that did not secure any protection of native rights would be a 'shameful peace'.

Kitchener, then, was not surprised when Botha broke off negotiations on 16 March. He simply applied himself even more vigorously to defeating the Boers by a series of 'drives' that would clear the veld of every living thing that could give suste-

nance to the Boers. There must be nowhere left for the guerrillas to hide.

It was at this time that questions were beginning to be asked in Britain about the concentration camps. This was due, in large measure, to a clergyman's daughter from Cornwall named Emily Hobhouse who had taken it upon herself to visit some of the camps in the Orange River Colony early in 1901. Labelled a 'pro-Boer', she had taken an active part on the South African Women and Children's Distress Fund when war broke out, and became increasingly alarmed by the reports coming out of the former Boer republics. As her great niece, Jennifer Hobhouse Balme, explains:

Just little scraps of information came across, and this was because of the censorship, and that made it very

Almost 28,000 white women and children died in the concentration camps.

worrying for everyone. Nobody knew quite what was happening. In fact Emily hadn't any idea of the number of camps until she got to South Africa.

Rina Viljoen's mother was in the Springfontein camp when Hobhouse began to make her visits:

My mother told me she often saw the hearse going past with sometimes up to thirteen corpses a day piled on the hearse as it went past. One day, my mother, the whole family, her brothers and sisters and my grandmother were sitting down to a family meal in the tent. Then they heard a voice outside. Suddenly a face peered into the tent and a voice asked: 'Everyone well?' After the arrival of Emily Hobhouse the conditions improved in the camp. There were not as many deaths any more.

Emily Hobhouse had been shocked by what she saw in the camps. The organization of such vast numbers of people clearly had not been thought through properly; food and medical supplies were woefully inadequate, sanitary provisions rarely included soap, and water supplies were under constant risk of pollution. To add insult to injury, the internees themselves were blamed for the squalid conditions in which they found themselves:

The theory put around was that the people were bad mothers and they weren't clean and, of course, they neglected their children and they used Dutch medicines which were folk medicines, and she felt that it was extremely unjust. Emily was devastated by the death rates, especially among the children. She loved children, she felt they were completely innocent. The women might support their husbands, but the children – the brunt of the war was on them.

Her tireless efforts to draw attention to the plight of the internees secured Emily Hobhouse a place in Afrikaner history, and this description of the death of a child, in one of her letters, forms the basis of a monument erected to commemorate the victims of the concentration camps:

The people massed there had no tents. Some crept under railway trucks, while others had begged bits of sailcloth from Tommies, and, sticking two or three sticks in the ground, threw canvas over them, making a rude shelter in which, however, they could seldom stand upright. In such a shelter I was called to see a sick baby. The mother sat on her little trunk, with the child across her knee. She had nothing to give it and the child was sinking fast…There was nothing to be done and we watched the child draw its last breath in reverent silence.

The mother neither moved nor wept, it was her only child. Dry-eyed but deathly white she sat there motionless looking not at the child but far far away into the depths of grief beyond all tears. A friend stood behind her who called upon Heaven to witness the tragedy and others crouching on the ground around her wept freely. The scene made an indelible impression on me.

Emily Hobhouse was about to make an indelible impression on the British army. Lord Kitchener had not really taken much notice of her when she had arrived in South Africa, along with the Quakers, Isabella and Joshua Rowntree. But she soon became a thorn in his side with her constant demands for improvements in the running of the camps. As Jennifer Hobhouse Balme relates, Hobhouse decided on another tactic in the face of Kitchener's intransigence:

She realized that she couldn't do anything more in South Africa, she had to go home and try and put pressure from the very top to try and get reforms and some proper arrangements. So she packed her bags and went back to London.

On returning to London, Hobhouse's family connections quickly secured her meetings with leading politicians and threw herself into drawing attention to the primitive conditions and rising mortality rates among the 60,000 Boers interned in the camps. The minister for war, St John Broderick, gave her a brief hearing but nothing more. So she approached the leader of the Liberal opposition, Sir Henry Campbell-Bannerman, and other anti-war politicians, including the Liberal firebrand, David Lloyd George. Campbell-Bannerman famously described the devastation of the land and concentration of people in camps as 'methods of barbarism', while Lloyd George accurately foresaw that:

A barrier of dead children's bodies will rise up between the British and the Boer races in South Africa.

In June 1901 St John Broderick was forced to defend the government's conduct of the war in the House of Commons. He argued that the extreme measures were necessary to combat the extreme guerrilla tactics of the Boers. As for the women in the camps, those who were not actively assisting the guerrillas had effectively been left to starve, and so the concentration camps were fulfilling a dual military and humanitarian function.

Although the government won the vote, the opposition, most notably Lloyd George, managed to demonstrate that the British government didn't really have a clue about the true picture of internment and mortality rates in South Africa.

The makeshift shelter of a black concentration camp with the tents of the white camp in the background.

Emily Hobhouse's intervention ensured that Kitchener and his camps were put under much closer scrutiny.

It took Emily Hobhouse all her energy to draw attention to the fact that white people were dying in their thousands. The blacks were less fortunate in being denied a similar champion for their cause. As the Barolong chief, Simon Makodi, puts it:

The blacks suffered much more than the whites. The whites had support and help from elsewhere, but we had no one to help us.

The success of Kitchener's anti-guerrilla strategy depended on turning the veld into a barren, inhospitable wilderness. This, of course, meant that it was not just the Boers who had to be removed. The Africans, too, watched as their cattle were slaughtered and their homes were burned. Kitchener ordered that black house servants should accompany their mistresses to the camp. Rose van Rensburg remembers:

There were quite a lot of blacks in Bethulie camp. They were very grateful for what the Boers did for them, because they did not have food and things, and through the Boers they got a little food. There weren't an awful lot of blacks, but there were quite a few with them in the camps – captured at the same time.

The reason why the black servants might have seemed grateful to the Boers was because food rations were not issued to them. They were dependent on sharing the already meagre portions allocated to their mistresses.

However, the overwhelming number of African internees were not taken to white camps but kept separately, often only short distances away. Emily Hobhouse makes it clear in March 1901 that she was aware of the existence of African camps but felt unable to do anything about them herself:

Is it generally known and realized at home that there are many large Native (coloured) camps dotted about? In my opinion these need looking into badly. I understand the death rate at the one at Bloemfontein to be very high and so also in other places – but I cannot possibly pay any attention to them myself. Why shouldn't the Society of Friends send someone if the War goes on, or the Aboriginees Protection?

As it turned out, a commission was sent later in the year to investigate the condition of the camps but, of the thirty-three camps the Fawcett Commission chose to visit, not one was black. Although the commission was in favour of the war and the way it was being prosecuted, its findings vindicated the stance taken by Emily Hobhouse, and its recommendations, although not implemented until early 1902, transformed conditions in the camps. A school system was introduced, and eventually the death rate fell to under two per cent. This was due, in no small part, to removing the camps from under the auspices of the military and transferring them to civilian control. Unfortunately, this all came far too late for the hundreds of thousands of women and children who had been interned since late 1900.

For Biebie van der Merwe there is a lasting reminder of the suffering experienced by her mother's family:

When her father came to the farm shortly after the family had been taken to the concentration camp, he walked all over the farm and there was absolutely nothing left. He had his young brother-in-law with him…so they picked up acorns from the farmyard. And they took an old hand plough which was still lying among the debris, and a distance away from the house they ploughed a piece of land, and planted the acorns. And today there is a beautiful forest of oak trees. A small reminder of the day he came to his farm and found all his possessions and his wife and children gone.

When Kitchener applied the pressure and the Boers became increasingly short of supplies, it was more often than not the blacks who were forced to replenish them from their own homes. Simon Makodi's Barolongs in the western Transvaal were particularly vulnerable:

When the Boers came to the people, you were afraid of them, you did not understand them and did not know their language…They just used to take things, they took blankets and took clothes and would give us their old torn clothes, and push our mothers around. And the horses and the cattle they just took and there was nothing you could say.

He goes on to explain that when the British started taking Africans to the camps, there was almost a sense of relief that the Boers would no longer be able to reach them:

These camps were a place of safety and they used to call them 'places of safety', because they felt safe and they were guarded, and there was no one who could come and take their things by force.

In the Orange River Colony, Dorah Ramothibe also remembers the arrival of the British as being a positive development for the blacks:

> The soldiers came. They came from Scotland. They came to help us. We lived in a camp. There was an army camp, and we lived in the tents. We were looked after by the Scots. We started relaxing, although not entirely, when the soldiers arrived. We started having a better life, even the food was better.

Anna Molakeng was particularly struck by the appearance of the Highland Regiments:

> The English [sic] came riding horses. The clothes they wore were like dresses, and they were brownish or reddish, they wore berets on their heads and they had big collars over their shoulders. There were trumpets that they had, they would blow their trumpets, 'Brrr...'. Their clothes were not like those of the Boers.

The British convinced many of the blacks taken to concentration camps that they were going to a place of safety.

She and her family were only just managing to scrape by with no men to provide for them. Being taken to a British camp at least meant that they knew where the next meal was coming from:

> They saw that we had nothing and had no food. Then they gave us some food to eat and they took us to their camps. We were struggling a lot. We didn't have clothes to wear, especially the women; they had nothing to cover themselves. Even the kids, they wore torn clothes and they were dirty. The Boers had killed our older men and our young boys and they took the others. The English came to stop all this from happening.

Although there may have been an initial sense of relief at the approach of the British, life would not in fact be any easier for many of the blacks were swept off the veld. At first, only the Orange River Colony had any kind of structured camps. Africans in the Transvaal were simply dumped along the railway lines and left to fend for themselves. Many of them ended up cleaning latrines and performing other menial duties in the white camps. Paul Skosana's mother at least made it to a camp, but it was a frightening experience nevertheless:

> At the farm they were taken by people they didn't know. They were taken to the camps. They had to walk and had no transport. At the camp, my mother was very scared. They were scared because they didn't know if the fathers were dead or not.

The number of homeless Africans became so large that a new body, the Department of Native Refugees, was established to deal with them. But their use rather than their welfare seemed to be the primary concern of the authorities. If the army could plunder this source of native labour, it could release the mine-workers it had currently seconded, and the production of gold could be resumed. There was another reason why the DNR came into being. The British government could not afford to feed all the people it had dispossessed and, without people working the land, a famine seemed inevitable. So a decision was taken to make African women and children self-supporting. New camps were set up near unoccupied Boer farms, and the internees were encouraged to grow their own food and crops. Although the policy reduced the food bills for the British, it still did not solve the food shortage for Anna Molakeng:

> When we were at the camp, we were given rotten porridge to eat; we did not like it, and it was tasteless. During that time, our grandmothers and mothers would go around and pick up locusts; the small locusts they would give us to eat. The war was bad for us and it was very difficult. We used to eat all sorts of food and insects just to be full, and some stuff we would dig from the ground and eat. We survived just like that.

But as in the white camps, many people did not survive:

> Many people died of hunger there. The older people managed to survive, but the children were weak and their knees were shaking. We did not see the corpses, and our grandmother would just tell us they were sleeping.

The black concentration camps fell victim to the same disease epidemics, squalid conditions and malnutrition, but unlike the white camps there were no nurses, and what doctors there were provided only medical 'advice' for extra money, rather than medical care. There was, however, nothing to differentiate the quality of suffering in the concentration camps, no matter what the colour of the internees. The latest research estimates that in the sixty-six black camps, somewhere in the region of 20,000 Africans died. In the more strictly documented white camps, almost 28,000 deaths were recorded.

It is strange, then, that the grief and outrage extended to the victims from the Boer camps has not even now reached the black South Africans who also died in their tens of thousands. Fransjohan Pretorius believes that there is a political reason for this:

> The suffering and deaths of the women and children in the concentration camps was an important cornerstone in the establishment of Afrikaner nationalism in the twentieth century. The white concentration camps were elevated to the only concentration camps in existence – to represent the sufferings and to unite the Afrikaner. The paradigm that was created in the twentieth century was the paradigm in which the suffering was only the suffering of the Afrikaner.

The final part of Lord Kitchener's plan to defeat the Boers by sweeping and scouring the country was put into place shortly after the failure of the Middelburg peace negotiations. He placed small fortified constructions, or blockhouses, within

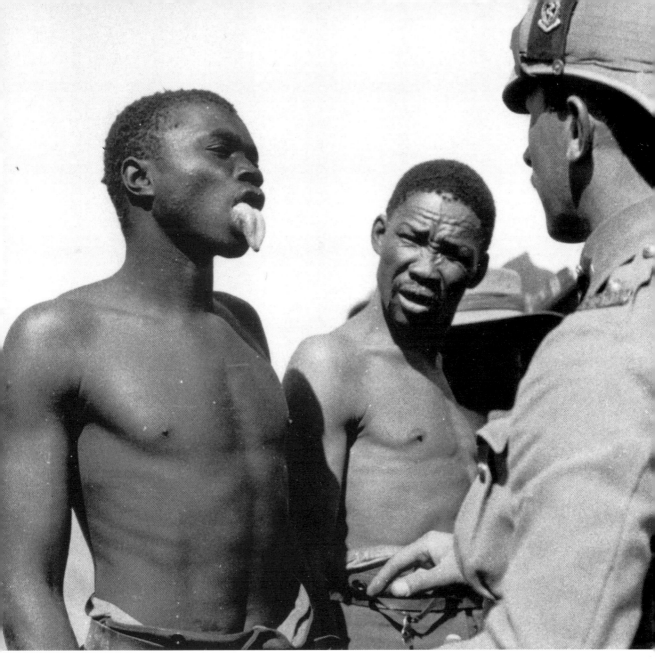

shooting range of each other and linked them together with telephones and, more important, barbed wire. By the end of the war 8,000 of these constructions had been built, spread over an area of 6,000 kilometres. Will Saxon wrote home from the Dunbar blockhouse:

I am in charge of the above mentioned blockhouse which is situated in a line of blockhouses extending

Fit black men were often used as cheap labour by the British army.

from Harrismith to De Beers. The BHs are places on eminences with from one to three miles distance between them. Our object is to prevent De Wet's commandos from breaking into Natal.

As he goes on to say, much of the work of con-

Armed black men were used by the British to man the blockhouses.

structing the blockhouses was performed by African labour, and at least 16,000 Africans were used as guards:

> I have been 'bossing' a number of 'niggers' who were doing all the muscular part of erecting defences along the Dunbar side of the line. We [the garrison] were kept busily employed all day till a barbed wire fence had been put up between our BH and the next.

Although the blockhouse system certainly slowed the Boers down, it came nowhere near to stopping them in their tracks. The guerrillas seemed to have an uncanny knack of spotting the weakest point in the blockhouse line and heading straight for it. Christiaan de Wet was still leading the British a merry dance, in spite of Kitchener's best efforts to run him into the ground. Trooper John Paterson of the Ayrshire Yeomanry is clearly disheartened as he writes home:

> I never knew what soldiering was till now. If the Sahara desert is any worse than this part of the world it must be bad. There is nothing but ostriches and goats and very few of either. The water is scarce and nearly always salt, and makes rotten tea. It was the worst thing De Wet ever did coming down here, I can see now why they let him through their lines so easy, but it has cost us terrible money in horseflesh.

The Boer fighting force had been whittled down until only those prepared to fight to the 'bitter end' were left. Fransjohan Pretorius describes the process:

> As the war progressed, and they suffered more and more personal losses – a home that was burned down, a wife and children taken to the concentration camps or a wife and children who died there – it happened he had nothing to go back to. And the mutual bond of the bitter-ender became strong in a group of burghers and it bound him in a core of fighting men, who were willing to give everything, because they had nothing else to go back to.

As the war dragged on, with no sign that the Boers would give up or that Kitchener was 'bagging' enough of them to claim victory, frustration on both sides turned into something altogether more vicious. The Boer General Kritzinger warned Kitchener that any blacks found working for the British, whether armed or not, would be executed. Kitchener sent a report to the War Office detailing several cases in which Africans had been shot by Boers:

> On or about 17th July, 1901, eight Kaffir boys, between the ages of 12 and 14, went out from Uitkijk, near Edenburg to get oranges. None were armed. Boers opened fire, shot one, captured six; one escaped, and is now with Major Damant. Corporal Willett, Damant's Horse, afterwards saw boys' bodies near farm, but so disfigured that they could not be recognized. Some Kaffirs were then sent out from Edenburg and recognized them…

The focus of the war moved to the Cape, and the Boers knew that this was their last chance to stir up any kind of significant Afrikaner rebellion. It was also mercifully free of blockhouses and barbed wire. Cape Colony under the British had extended the franchise to all men who had reached a certain level of literacy and income regardless of the colour of their skin. Many black and coloured people in the Cape believed that a British victory was the only way of keeping and perhaps extending their political rights. This allegiance proved a serious threat to the Boers. They realized that if the British succeeded in persuading the Cape coloureds and Africans to fight with them, the guerrillas would never succeed in establishing a foothold. The stakes were high, and as Republican law was instigated in Boer-occupied areas, non-white resistance to Republican incursions into the Cape was sometimes brutally suppressed.

Abraham Esau was a blacksmith from Calvinia in the north-western Cape. He was a resolutely pro-British leader of the local coloured community and spent much of his time rallying coloured support to the British flag. His great-niece Rachel Smith described his activities after the Boers occupied Calvinia in early 1901:

> Well, he went about among the people and he told them that the English came to save us from the burgher and they must now club together, we must now stand together and fight the burgher because they've got that Boer attitude towards the coloureds. And it is time to stand up for our rights.

The liberal presence of British missionaries in the western Cape

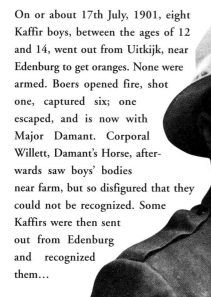

General P.H. Kritzinger invaded the Cape Colony but was forced back.

added to the perception of the British as being sympathetic towards the coloured situation:

> Well, the English were closer to the coloured people, they would come into your home and they would talk to you, they would eat from your plate whereas the burgher would never ever have done that. And also the English people would let you come in by their front door. With the burgher you had to go and knock at the kitchen door, you may not come in at the front door.

The fact of a coloured man blatantly supporting the British and feeding them with intelligence was too much for the Boers to countenance. They had already imposed their own Free State laws on the natives, significantly curtailing their rights, but Esau could not be cowed. He was duly arrested and sentenced to twenty-five lashes. But as Rachel Smith remembers, his punishment did not simply end there:

> He was dragged between two horses and then he was shot...And they told us, the children, that they cut out his tongue and they cut out Abraham Esau's eyes. There was still blood the next day where his blood had

Above: Gideon Scheepers (in a hat to the left) was one of several prominent Boers who was tried for the ill-treatment and execution of loyal blacks.
Opposite: Blacks loyal to the British often faced appalling brutality at the hands of Boers, like this man tied to a wagon wheel to be flogged.

been spilled. Then some of the people went to put flowers where Abraham Esau's blood was...

The story of Abraham Esau's treatment at the hands of the Boers was seized on by the British. He was, as Sir Alfred Milner put it, 'born and bred a British subject' and his punishment had stemmed from 'the offence of being loyal to the British Crown'. Esau took on the status of martyr to the British cause, and money was given to help build a little chapel to commemorate him.

But the politics of race in twentieth-century South Africa meant that the chapel would not be the lasting memorial the people had intended, as Rachel Smith explains:

> The Nationals got to power in 1948 and of course the main thing was apartheid – the races had got to be

separated. So we coloureds were zoned in a certain area, the whites were in another area, and the blacks were in another area. Unfortunately, our little chapel fell into the white area so we were given notice we had to vacate the place, and the church was then demolished...

Atrocities were not confined to the Boer side. In a diary entry from 1901, Walker Henderson Thomson from the Australian Bushman Corps brings home the gradual erosion of even the most basic rules of conduct in war:

> In charging a Boer position one day with bayonets their captain called out not to kill that man as he was a field cornet. Don't give a — if he is a whole brass band howled Pat as he ran him through.
>
> Guards over the Boers get very tired sometimes and treat the Boers very well. One instance of it is the M. Fusiliers were very tired after a long march and it was very cold and wet so they thought it would be easier to mind corpses than live men so they bayoneted about thirty of the Boers and lay down and had a good sleep.

That was not a unique occurrence. Lieutenant 'Breaker' Morant and Lieutenant Handcock of the Bushveldt Carbineers were famously and controversially executed for ordering the shooting of twelve Boer prisoners. Their defence, to the charge of twelve counts of murder, was that shooting prisoners was, by then, standard practice.

Major John Buist's father was present at the execution of Gideon Scheepers, a commandant of the republican forces fighting in the eastern Cape, who had been found guilty of committing capital crimes against both British soldiers and unarmed coloureds:

> Among these coloured people was a young girl who was pregnant and she was tied to the wheel of a wagon and thrashed until she gave birth under the lash.

The veld was a terrifying and dangerous place to be during the guerrilla war no matter who you were. In December 1901, in what turned out to be one of the most effective counterguerrilla measures of the war, Kitchener issued orders that unless they were starving, women and children were no longer to be taken to the camps, but were to be left on the veld. The responsibility for their welfare now rested with the guerrillas. To look after their families meant sacrificing both their mobility and their invisibility. To leave them behind meant leaving them unprotected in an increasingly hostile environment. The Free State burgher Roland Schikkerling noted in his diary:

> The natives, of whom there are millions northwards, have of late become very bold, and have now in some parts waged open war on us...Our women who are still on the farms are becoming terrified and indeed they have reason to be when one recalls the horrifying treatment received by them in earlier days from these savages.

But it was not just white women who were at risk. According to Moruti Setiloane, his father witnessed the gang rape of an African woman in the Orange River Colony:

> There came this troop of Johnnies – English soldiers on horseback. There was this woman there who was gathering cow dung, dry cow dung to go and make fire. And as they came on, there she was. Naturally like men who had been away from women, they were sex starved, they came and they pushed her rough and they raped her. And he tells about how she lay there and one would go into her and go over and another one would come into her and go over, and every time, and somebody went, she laid with her arms open, they would fish out a note with the Queen's head and put it on her hand. That is the fairness of the British, you've got to pay for what you get.

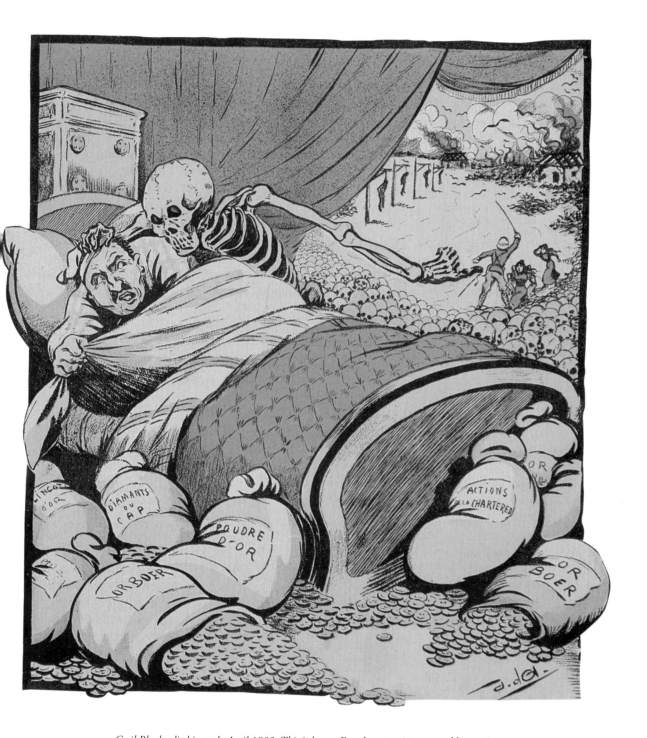

Cecil Rhodes died in early April 1902. This is how a French cartoonist mourned his passing.

One of the most notorious atrocities of the war was committed by Manie Maritz's father Gerhardus, also known as Manie. Leliefontein was a Methodist mission station in Namaqualand, and Maritz went there to demand that the European missionaries did not become involved in the war. As in many other districts in the Cape, the coloured population had been helping the British, and they did not respond well when Maritz issued a decree forbidding them, on pain of death, to continue to do so. As Manie Maritz junior describes:

> My father went to them and said, 'Look, this story of you supporting the English, we don't want this. We will not bother you, but we do not want you to come and put forward your shit here. We will give you a proclamation and tell you under what circumstances you may live here.' And they read it to them, and when they got to the point where General Maritz said 'I do not want you to fight in the war, or fight for the Queen of England', Barnabas Links said 'You bastard, don't you speak that way about my Queen', and he hit him over his head with a knobkerrie.

The official version is that when the ultimatum – Republican loyalty or death – was read out, the assembled villagers became restless. A man called Barnabas Links was in the crowd and he started to shout at Maritz. Maritz produced his *sjambok*, and Links went for him with a stick, or knobkerrie. The crowd surged forward and the mounted Boer commando fired directly into them. Armed Leliefontein men responded in kind and Maritz beat a hasty retreat to the

General Manie Maritz wiped out the entire coloured settlement of Leliefontein in the Cape.

hills, but not before being ambushed and losing thirty of his men.

Maritz and what was left of his commando would not let Leliefontein get the better of them, as his son recounts:

> The next day they went back to put the coloured people in their place. My father always said that it was war, and they went there to teach those people a lesson; and that was the point of having gone to Leliefontein.

The lesson was a brutal one. Deneys Reitz, who was now in the Cape with General Jan Smuts, rode into Leliefontein shortly after Maritz had left:

> We found the place sacked and gutted, and among the rocks beyond the burned houses lay twenty or thirty dead Hottentots…To avenge the insult, he [had] returned next morning with a stronger force and wiped out the settlement, which seemed to many of us a ruthless and unjustifiable act.

According to his son, Maritz's actions at the mission station drove a wedge between him and Smuts:

> General Smuts stood there watching and shook his head saying that…as if to say Manie Maritz is an unreasonable man; he didn't say it, but anyone who looked at him could read that this was what he was thinking. And that caused a great tension between Maritz and Smuts, because Maritz said "Would Smuts have felt better if twenty Afrikaners were lying dead there in place of twenty coloureds who are lying dead there?". And that was the cause of the tension between the two of them.

That tension would find its most extreme expression during the First World War. Maritz defected to the German side and led a rebellion of Boer troops which was finally crushed by Botha and Smuts, who by that time had become Imperial statesmen.

Guerrilla war in the Cape dragged on with no decisive result for either side. Smuts' commandos were able to inflict a bloody surprise on Lord Vivian and the Seventeenth Lancers at Elands River Poort – not least because many of the Boers were wearing khaki. The guerrillas restocked and rearmed, and the British reissued the orders that any Boer found in a British uniform would be shot on sight.

The score was evened when a British column led by Sir Harry Scobell successfully attacked and destroyed one of the most effective Boer commandos in the Cape led by Commandant Lotter.

As Smuts penetrated deeper into the Cape, Louis Botha began his journey towards Natal to see if an Afrikaner rebellion could be raised there. He was met by Major Gough's military infantry at Blood River Poort, but turned the tables on them and inflicted a humiliating defeat which left Gough limping, horseless and barefoot, back to safety.

But Botha's luck did not hold out, and after a futile attempt to wrest more supplies from two British camps his men were forced to retreat back into the Transvaal.

Kitchener's focus could now return to Christiaan De Wet, who had concentrated a large group of guerrillas in the Orange River Colony. 20,000 men were assigned the task of hunting De Wet down including newly formed National Scouts made up of Boers fighting for the British.

After De Wet had successfully carried out a daring raid on the British camp at Tweefontein on Christmas Day 1901, Kitchener determined to run De Wet into the ground. Vast columns of men would drive De Wet against the lines of blockhouses and barbed wire. There would be nowhere for him to run.

But with a pair of wire-clippers De Wet snipped through the wire of the Kroonstad-Lindley line and confounded Kitchener's plans once more.

Kitchener's second drive also failed, and his third saw De Wet managing to get through three blockhouse lines. From his blockhouse, Will Saxon wrote:

> I wish your mother had that Yorkshire pudding ready for me when I came out of the trenches at daybreak after spending the night waiting for De Wet & his merrie men. By the time this letter reaches home you will have heard of Kitchener's Drive. We the Manchester Vols held an active and responsible position holding the part of the blockhouse line from which the Boers recoiled. Over 1,100 Boers were captured. Innumerable cattle &c have been driven through our lines during the last few days. From the 24th to the 27th Feb we have stood all night in trenches waiting for the Boers (nice warm nights). Several commandants have been taken but the slippery De Wet escaped once more…

Things got worse at Tweebosch on 7 March 1902 when Lord Methuen's column met Koos de la Rey. As well as losing six big guns and almost all of his column, Lord Methuen himself was taken prisoner. Despite this victory, the Boers had nowhere left to go. Their men were tired, their women were in danger, and all attempts at raising an Afrikaner rebellion in either the Cape or Natal had failed.

Cecil Rhodes had died in March 1902, and Queen Victoria had been buried at the beginning of 1901. Neither of them lived to see the moment when the Boers decided that they wanted to talk about ending the war.

The troops returned from South Africa having been taught,
as Kipling put it, 'no end of a lesson'.

CHAPTER SEVEN

'A Shameful Peace'

I truly believe that if there is war again the people of the Transvaal
will assist the Boers…The natives of the Transvaal say 'we expected
deliverance whereas we have gone deeper into bonds'.

SEGALE, A BAKGATLA CHIEF, WRITING IN 1903

O N 15 MAY 1902 THE sixty elected
Boer delegates arrived at Vereeniging
to discuss whether to accept
Kitchener's peace terms. Both former
republics had been provided with a tent, and there
was a huge marquee for the joint discussion. The
attitude of the delegates was also split into two
camps, with the Transvaal generally favouring
submission and the Orange Free State preferring to
carry on with the fight. Louis Botha summarized
the case for ending the war: there was an acute
shortage of food and horses; women and children
were suffering even more now they were being left
on the veld instead of being taken to concentration
camps; there was no realistic prospect of a Cape
rebellion or help from abroad; and Kitchener's
blockhouse system was proving increasingly effective in restricting the Boers' movements. Even Koos
de la Rey agreed that the bitter end had come and
that they should take the opportunity to negotiate.

Christiaan de Wet, however, believed their
position was no worse than it had been when they
had rejected the Middelburg terms. This struggle
was the will of God, and they should continue to
fight. After days of argument, the convention
decided that the five representatives – Louis
Botha, Jan Smuts and Schalk Burger for the
Transvaal, and Christiaan de Wet and Barry
Hertzog for the Free State – would offer Kitchener
a compromise deal in which the republics would
enter into a 'defensive alliance' with Great Britain
but remain independent.

On 19 May the Boer leaders resumed their talks
with the British at Kitchener's house in Pretoria.
The compromise was put forward by Smuts and
Hertzog but, unsurprisingly, was rejected by the
British. Kitchener's instructions from the Cabinet
had always been to stick closely to the terms
offered at Middelburg while conceding an
amnesty for the Cape rebels. The notion of the

Boers somehow retaining their independence was completely out of the question.

Despite Sir Alfred Milner's complete unwillingness to make any concessions to the Boers, and De Wet's conviction that the war should not be prematurely brought to a halt, Kitchener and Smuts managed to keep the talks going long enough to hammer out a proposal for peace terms. They were essentially the same as those offered by the British at Middelburg, but there were three important concessions. Firstly, none of the Cape rebels except for the leaders would face imprisonment; secondly the question of the native franchise in the former Boer republics would not be considered

Above: *At the peace talks of Vereeniging Christiaan de Wet wanted to continue the guerrilla campaign against the British.*
Opposite: *De Wet was finally persuaded by Louis Botha and Koos de la Rey to give up the fight.*

until after representative government had been introduced; and thirdly the amount of money offered to help rebuild the country would be trebled from £1 million to £3 million.

The terms were given the blessing of the British Cabinet, and the Boer leaders returned to Vereeniging to put them to the delegates.

Back in February 1900 the British Prime Minister, Lord Salisbury, had said:

> There must be no doubt…that due precaution will be taken for the kindly and improving treatment of those countless indigenous races of whose destiny I fear we have been too forgetful.

A dose of collective amnesia had clearly overwhelmed the Cabinet then, when they effectively allowed for the minority group in a self-governing Boer state to determine whether or not the majority group of black Africans should get the vote. As Moruti Setiloane points out, it certainly gave the lie to the notion that Britain had gone to war with the Boers in part to secure native rights in the two republics:

> And after all the glory and praise and hype about Queen Victoria and her fairness, you see, when then they were talking about a treaty with the Boers, not only were the blacks not there, but even the interests of blacks were not represented.

On 29 May the Boer representatives arrived back at Vereeniging and went straight to the tent of the Free State's President Steyn. He had been too ill to take part in the Pretoria negotiations but was implacably opposed to any thoughts of stopping the war. When he saw the draft terms of surrender he immediately resigned his presidency in disgust. This left De Wet as the main spokesman for the continuance of the war. He was adamant that it was still feasible to continue the struggle – even the

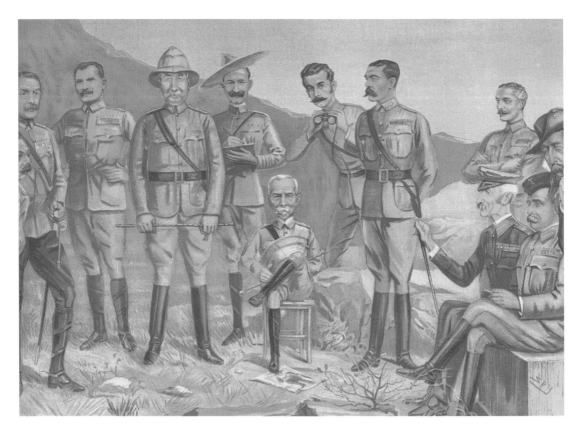

This cartoon shows Lord Roberts (seated), Sir Redvers Buller (third from left), Baden-Powell (fourth from left), and Kitchener (fifth from right).

suffering of the women and children on the veld should be seen as a 'necessary circumstance' of the fight for independence.

The British had given the Boers until midnight on 31 May to get a simple yes or no to the terms, and time was running out. On the morning of the thirty-first Botha and De la Rey made a final appeal to De Wet, urging him to see that they could not possibly win the war but that they now had a chance to win the peace. Their plea to De Wet was successful, and after drawing up a summary document of why the British terms should be accepted, the delegates were asked to vote.

The six reasons given in the document were that the scorched-earth policy had made it impossible to carry on; the concentration camps were inflicting terrible sickness and suffering on the population; the African tribes were also waging war against them, as evidenced by the Vryheid massacre; proclamations that burghers would have their land confiscated would lead to utter ruin; they had no means of keeping prisoners of war; and there was no realistic chance of victory.

Fighting in relatively isolated guerrilla units, most men had only a very local sense of how the war was progressing. The discussions at Vereeniging changed all that, revealing the stark reality of the Boer situation for the first time.

In the early afternoon of 31 May, a vote was

taken accepting Kitchener's terms by fifty-four votes to six. By 11.05 a.m. the Boer leaders had sped back to Pretoria, and the Peace of Vereeniging had been signed by Kitchener, Milner, Burger and De Wet. As Kitchener shook hands with the Boers he said, 'We are good friends again now' – a sentiment that Lesobe Phaladi, the Bakgatla whose father had helped the British in the north-west Transvaal, believes to have had a certain inevitability:

> There is a saying, 'When brothers fight, never intervene'. In English they normally say 'blood is thicker than water'. So the English people together with the Boers made friends again.

Now the delegates had the unenviable job of going back to tell their men in the field that

Boer leaders like De Wet had the difficult task of telling their men of the British victory. Having fought for so long, the Boers found the news difficult to accept.

the Boers had surrendered their independence. For Manie Maritz's father it was a bitter pill to swallow:

> They say that in the morning he got on to his horse and he rode around the fields like someone possessed. He was afraid that there would be peace, and he did not know how to deal with that. There was a great animosity when General Smuts came back and he said that they had made peace. Because the people did not want peace, they said that if you fight for freedom, then only death should separate you and your freedom.

Roland Schikkerling listened as General Viljoen described the difficulty of coming to the decision at Vereeniging:

> He tells us he hopes never again to be called on to perform so sad a duty. He saw stern and rugged men rise to speak. Yet, before they could utter many words, they were choked with emotion and had to wipe away their tears.

But that did not lessen the intense disappointment felt by his men. On the day he learned of the surrender, Schikkerling wrote:

> Think of it. After fighting for thirty-two months against such odds and after keeping alive the flame of freedom for so long, to hand up our arms, forfeit that independence so dear to us, yield up this fair country, lose our separate existence, and become merged in that of the conqueror!…To me everything in which hope was, seems gone, and I feel as if our liberty has been buried alive and our future stillborn.

Being steeped in religion, the Boers also had to come to terms with the fact that the maintenance of two independent Boer republics in South Africa was clearly not part of the divine plan. According

Below: *The 'bitter enders' gained a place in Afrikaner legend for their tenacious struggle against Kitchener's drives, the blockhouse system and the overwhelming numerical superiority of the British Army.*
Opposite: *In South Africa today there is probably as much hatred towards the 'joiners' – Boers who fought for the British – than towards the British themselves.*

to Professor Fransjohan Pretorius, the British victory was the ultimate test of their faith:

> When the burghers in the veld heard that they had lost their independence, some of them, with fists raised to the sky, shouted: 'I have lost my faith.' And some burghers spoke to God and they said: 'Was there not one righteous man? What did we do to lose our independence?'

But others, like General Maritz's son Manie, believe that the reasons for the Boers' defeat are altogether more secular:

> We would not have lost if we had somewhere to keep our prisoners of war. And another factor was the traitors in our midst. We would have won this war, the war we Boers fought for three years. And if the English hadn't murdered 27,000 women and children, we also could have won the war. But when they couldn't beat the men, the English attacked the women and children.

Hendryk Swanepoel's uncle Johannes was a hands-upper:

> He did not want to fight any more. It is just like my grandfather said: a farmer can only fight for three months. He then wants to get back to his farming…and he knew the battle was lost. That is why he laid down his weapon and surrendered to the English.

21,000 Boers remained fighting to the bitter end, but no fewer than one-fifth of all Afrikaners fighting at the end of the war were in fact fighting on the British side.

For Rina Viljoen's father, the primary cause of the Boer defeat was the behaviour of the joiners:

He used to say that because of all the traitors, the Boers lost the war. If only there were fewer traitors. Everything was too disorganized, too little discipline. No one wanted to follow. Everyone just wanted to do his own thing.

Marie Proudfoot feels even more strongly:

Do you know what a joiner is? He is a bedbug who should be squashed to death. That's what he is – bedbug. Kill him. Afterwards the joiner suffered just as much as the others because there was no income. What did it help them to join? Nothing!

In fact, that was not strictly true. The joiners fared much better with their compensation claims that followed the war than the ordinary burghers.

Rina Viljoen's mother had been in the Springfontein concentration camp for fourteen months when news came that something momentous had happened:

And then one day a pastor arrived. He was running past their tent shouting: 'Peace! Peace!' Everyone was running after him. But no one knew what kind of a peace it was: did the English [sic] or the Boers win the war? Everyone was just running. They all went to find

After the war ended, many families had to remain in the camps until they could be transported back to their homes.

out what had happened. Who had won the war? And there they heard that peace was declared and that the English [sic] had won the war.

But many of the internees were miles from home and could not just walk out of the gates. Rina Viljoen's mother and surviving relatives had to stay in the camp for several months after the peace settlement, waiting for transport back to their farm:

> Eventually they obtained a wagon that could take them back to their farmstead. They also received some provisions, but it was too little to sustain them. The oxen that pulled the wagon were so emaciated and so slow that the children and the women had to get off the wagon and walk alongside. And so they went back to the farm.

The same scenes of slow dispersal were being played out at the black camps as well. In most cases, black internees could only leave the camps when they were 'claimed' by a white employer. Far from fulfilling the expectation, and sometimes even the explicit promise, that they could take over the Boer farms they had been working, black families found themselves in exactly the same position that they had been in before the war. But as Anna Molakeng remembers, two years was a long time out of her life:

> Some people did not remember where they came from. I was in the camps from the

time I was a small child, and when I left the camp I was beginning to mature and my breasts had developed already, and when we left the camp we didn't even remember where our homes were.

Although the war had come to an end, the suffering continued for many of the men who went to look for their families in the concentration camps. Marie Proudfoot describes the scene:

> You know there are people who, when they arrived at the camps, everybody in their families were dead. There was nobody – no child, no wife, nobody. They signed the peace, nobody was left...The man would stand there with his hat on his head and his horse at his arm...he would look for them. 'Where are they?' And somebody would say, 'Over there in the cemetery.' Those poor women.

The British scorched-earth policy had successfully laid waste to most of the Transvaal and the Orange River Colony. The intention had been to remove all forms of sustenance from the guerrillas, but an inevitable consequence was that it was also removed from the families who were now returning to their homes to attempt to rebuild their lives.

Sir Alfred Milner and a group of ambitious young men from Oxford known as 'the kindergarten' had already begun a process of reconstruction, but it had not, as yet, extended much further than the Rand. Gold production had been taken in hand and, by a stringent application of the pass laws and tight control over the cost of African labour, Milner had managed to increase the output from 7,400

No black south African would agree that there had been 'Peace with Honour.'

ounces in May 1901 to 120,000 ounces in April 1902. This was certainly a feather in the cap of the kindergarten, but it did not go any way to helping the families of people like Marie Proudfoot when they returned:

> When they got out of the camp, they had to go to the farm, and what did they find there? A burned-down farmhouse with corrugated-iron sheets all curled up. Where were they supposed to live? Under the empty skies without food, without anything.

Rose van Rensburg's family returned to the veld to find nothing but charred remains where their home had once been:

> After the war my mother was of course very bitter, but

When families finally left the camps they returned to scenes of devastation like this one.

she was very glad that peace had come at last, and she just felt thankful that it was all over, that they could now start a new life. But that wasn't so easy. What few possessions they owned, the English had thrown on to their cart and burned. This was a terrible source of grievance – that what little they had was burned.

The more fortunate women, like Abrie Oosthuizen's grandmother, no longer had to face such hardships on their own. Long-absent hus-bands returned from the war to take over their tra-ditional roles as protectors and providers:

> The group of women on the station embraced their husbands and cried, and it was a terrible scene. But my grandmother was a tiger of a woman, and she went to him, 'Gideon, don't just stand there sobbing, come to the farm. There's work to be done.'

It was not just the women who had to readjust to

having a man around again. Children were reunited with fathers they had not seen for years. Marie Proudfoot's grandfather was almost unrecognizable when he returned to his family:

> When my grandmother told them that that man there is your father who came back, they just stood there astounded because Grandfather had a huge beard hanging there. And he looked terribly ragged, with his rifle over his shoulder and his hat on his head. Three years he was away in the bushes and in the veld.

The war in South Africa between 1899 and 1902 exacted a high cost from all those willingly, and unwillingly, caught up in it. For the British, the war they had embarked on, confidently expecting to win with 75,000 men, required close to 450,000. The three months they thought it would take to put the Boers in their place took almost three years. Almost 22,000 British and colonial troops died fighting for the British Empire, 16,000 of these perishing not from wounds but from disease. The mules, horses and donkeys that died during the conflict numbered almost half a million.

It is estimated that of the 88,000 men who fought on the Boer side, 7,000 were killed. 28,000 non-combatants died in the concentration camps, the vast majority of them small children. Countless homes were destroyed, and several million cattle, horses and sheep were slaughtered or stolen.

The African death toll is harder to calculate as many deaths went unrecorded. The latest research estimates that of the 115,000 blacks interned in concentration camps, 20,000 died. There were also blacks who were summarily shot by the Boers if they were suspected of helping the British, and those who were killed while performing their duties as scouts and *agterryers*.

After much prevarication, Lord Kitchener finally admitted to arming more than 10,000 Africans. In the House of Commons, the Liberal MP David Lloyd George suggested the number lay closer to 30,000. The true figure probably lies somewhere between the two. What cannot be disputed is the contribution made by black Africans to the British war effort. Lesobe Phaladi still feels the injustice of the peace settlement between the British and the Boers:

> It was not good because when the war was over we did not get anything. The English gave land to the Boers and nothing to us, and that was very unfair because we all fought in this war.

The sense of having been used simply as pawns by the whites was increased when all black people in the Transvaal were made to surrender their arms and ammunition:

> When they took the guns from the black people, the Boers said that there would be war again and the guns had to be taken away from the blacks because they were a strong nation. The people took the guns to the chiefs, and they took guns from the chiefs. That is how it happened.

Moruti Setiloane, whose father had helped General Cronje's wife escape from the Transvaal, makes it clear that the Africans who had supported the Boer war effort also felt betrayed by the whites they had supported:

> Before the war the people lived together, they worked their lands together. Then after the war there came the big tragedy of the divide. When they had helped the Afrikaner, the Boer to win the war, thinking that it was their own war too, and when

For decades the history books colluded in an attempt to maintain the notion of the 'white man's war'.

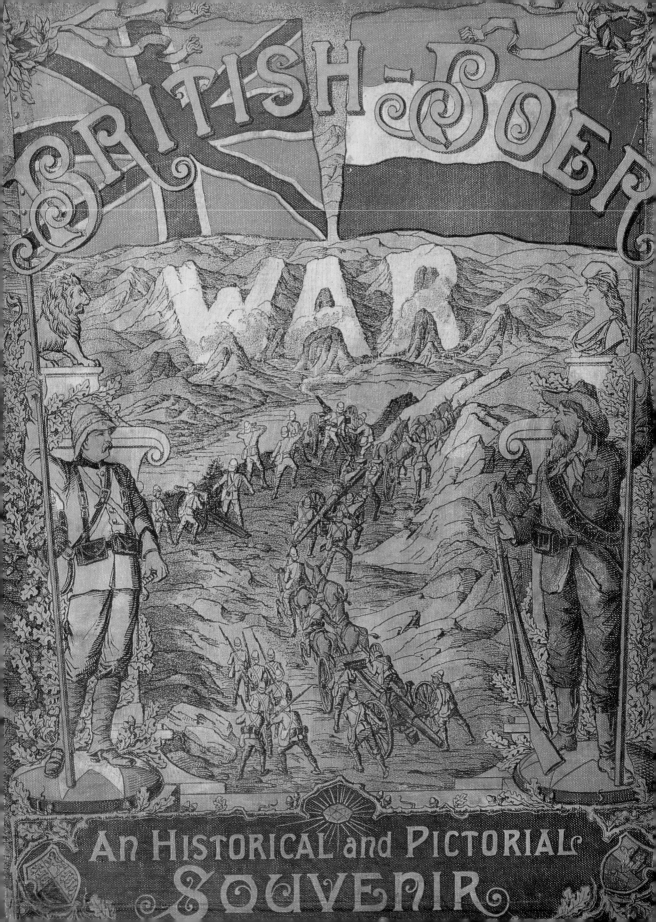

BRITISH-BOER WAR

An Historical and Pictorial Souvenir

the spoils of the war came in the union of South Africa, they were sidelined and they were pushed out. This is where the African people feel that they were sold out by the Boers at the time.

Within a decade, South Africa was a self-governing dominion of the British Empire. Firstly, under Henry Campbell-Bannerman, who had condemned Kitchener's 'methods of barbarism', the Crown Colonies of the Transvaal and the Orange River Colony were given the right to govern themselves. Then, in 1910, Natal, Cape Colony, the Transvaal and the renamed Orange Free State were brought together to form the Union of South Africa. Louis Botha was the first Prime Minister.

The question of who won the war in South Africa is not as straightforward as military history would make it appear. If the Boer republics went to war in the name of liberty, then in the long term they were successful. Self-government was granted within a couple of years of losing the war, and majority Boer governments had been elected by 1908. A fully independent Republic of South

The Boers may not have won the war but they had certainly won the peace.

Africa was created in 1961, on the fifty-ninth anniversary of the Peace of Vereeniging.

It is clearer to see who lost the war. Article 8 of the peace terms sealed the fate of black political rights for almost a hundred years. By postponing the question of the native franchise until after the republics had become self-governing, Great Britain effectively rubber-stamped the disenfranchisement of the majority of the population. The issue was on the table once more in 1909 when the Union of South Africa was being discussed, but again the British approved the incorporation of the colour bar into the constitution. Claims that the British were fighting for equality between 1899 and 1902 do not sit easily with their role in overseeing the foundations of apartheid.

During the two world wars, the Union of South Africa fought for the British Empire. Louis Botha and Jan Smuts reconciled themselves to the imperial project to the extent of suppressing an armed Boer rebellion led by Christiaan de Wet and Manie Maritz's father. But in 1948 Daniel Malan's National Party replaced Jan Smuts' more liberal anglicized administration. The rise to power of the National Party was part of the process in which the Afrikaner was reinvented. According to Fransjohan Pretorius:

> History constantly walks along, looking over its shoulder at the Anglo-Boer War – what happened there? The Anglo-Boer War became a time for the creation of myths for the Afrikaners.

As Fransjohan Pretorius makes clear, the Boer War provided the historical backdrop against which Afrikaners could define themselves as a nation forged through war out of suffering:

> Three things are important: capitalism that flooded us and took our independence away; the concentration camps that caused terrible suffering among our people; and thirdly the heroic deeds during the war – the great victories, the famous generals. And these three factors, the anti-capitalism, the suffering and death in the concentration camps and the heroism of the Boers during the war, were used to unite the Afrikaners and give them back their pride.

But the rewriting of history to exclude the blacks from both the terrible suffering and the heroic deeds of the war is something that still angers Moruti Setiloane:

> What gets one really worked up today is when the Afrikaner wants to make as if he is the only one who lost in the Boer War and forgets that the black man shared as much of his riches, of his livelihood, and even of his blood – I lost my two uncles in the Boer War. And now, whenever people speak about the Boer War they speak of it as if it was a war of the Boers

alone against the English, when actually it was a war of the people of South Africa against the English.

As the new South Africa of fully democratic rule struggles unsteadily to its feet, it must take into account people like Manie Maritz who are still prepared to fight for the liberty of the Afrikaner:

> For a Maritz to lose his freedom is worse than death. We trekked from the Cape, and we were absolutely freedom crazy. That was all we fought for, and that's what we lived for. So if it was Gerhard Maritz in 1836; Manie Maritz in 1902; or if it was me in 1998, the freedom of the Afrikaner volk is the most important thing that we live for. And if we cannot get it, then we will be prepared go to war for it if we have to.

But not all Afrikaners feel the same way. For Abrie Oosthuizen, the Boer War has, in a historical sense at least, united the Afrikaner and the black African:

> If you ask me now about the fingerprints it left on my life I would say it gave me an enormous pride as an Afrikaner. That we went through those things and survived it and as a nation we came through – with all our shortcomings…The sorrow inflicted upon us in the Boer War, which was actually a common factor between us and the blacks, is something that ties me to the black people in this country. In the greatest sorrow that my nation suffered, they were co-sufferers in concentration camps and they went through the same stuff that my people went through.

Perhaps the last word should go to the Barolong chief, Simon Makodi:

> I feel that we must all live together in peace, so that when we die we leave our children in the light and the truth where all of us live together.

Sources

Noel Coward said that reading a footnote was like having to go downstairs to answer the door while in the middle of making of love. Without wishing to make any claims for the satisfaction this book may give its reader I have provided a list of plundered source material rather than footnotes. Special mention must go to Thomas Pakenham's masterpiece *The Boer War* and to the exhaustive *Times History of the War in South Africa*.

Primary Sources

Churchill, Winston, *London to Ladysmith via Pretoria* (Location: Longmans & Co., 1900).

De Wet, Christiaan, *Three Years War* (Westminster: Archibald Constable & Co Ltd., 1902).

Emerson Neilly, J., *Besieged with B-P* (London: C.A. Pearson, 1900).

Hamilton, Angus, *The Siege of Mafeking* (London: Methuen, 1900).

Hancock, W.K., *Smuts Vol 1: The Sanguine Years 1870–1919* (Cambridge: Cambridge University Press, 1962).

MacDonald, Donald, *How We Kept the Flag Flying: The Story of the Siege of Ladysmith* (London: Ward Lock, 1900).

Peach, Victor, *By Jingo: Letters from the Veldt* (Totness: Totness Community Archive, 1987).

Pemberton, W.B., *Battles of the Boer War* (London: B.T. Batsford, 1964).

Pen Pictures of the War by men at the front (London: H. Marshall & Son, 1900).

Phillipps, L. March, *With Rimington* (London: Edward Arnold, 1902).

Plaatje, Sol, *Mafeking Diary* (Cambridge: Meridon, 1990).

Plaatje, Sol, *Native Life in South Africa* (London: Publisher, 1916).

Ralph, Julian, *War's Brighter Side: the story of The Friend newspaper* (London: Arthur Pearson, 1901).

Reitz, Deneys, *Commando* (London: Faber and Faber, 1929)

Schikkerling, R.W., *Commando Courageous (A Boer's Diary)* (Johannesburg: Keartland, 1964).

Steevens, G.W. *From Capetown to Ladysmith* (London: W. Blackwood & Sons, 1900).

Secondary Sources

Amery, L.S. (Ed), *The Times History of the War in South Africa* (London: Sampson, Low & Co., 1909).

Faber, Richard, *The Vision and the Need: Late Victorian Imperialist Aims* (London: Faber & Faber, 1966).

Hillcourt, W. & O. Baden-Powell, Baden-Powell: *The Two Lives of a Hero* (London: Heinemann, 1964).

Jeal, Tim, *Secondary Sources: Baden-Powell* (London: Pimlico, 1991).

Kruger, Rayne, *Goodbye Dolly Gray* (London: Pimlico, 1959).

Lee, Emanoel, *To The Bitter End* (London: Viking, 1985).

Pakenham, Thomas, *The Boer War* (London: Abacus, 1992).

Pretorius, Fransjohan, *On Commando* (to be published 1999).

Smith, I.R., *The Origins of the South African War* (London: Longman, 1996).

Sparks, Allister, *The Mind of South Africa* (London: Heinemann, 1990).

Spies, S. B., *Methods of Barbarism* (Cape Town: Human & Rousseau, 1977).

van Reenen, Rykie, *Boer War Letters: Emily Hobhouse* (Cape Town: Human and Rousseau, 1977).

van Wyk Smith, Malvern, *Drummer Hodge: the Poetry of the Anglo-Boer War* (Oxford: Oxford University Press, 1978).

Warwick, Peter (Ed), *The South African War* (London: Longman, 1980).

Warwick, John *Black People and the South African War 1899–1902*, (Cambridge: Cambridge University Press, 1983).

Wessel, André, *The Phases of the Anglo-Boer War* (Bloemfontein: War Museum of the Boer Republics, 1998).

Wheatcroft, Geoffrey, *The Randlords* (New York: Weidenfeld & Nicolson, 1985).

Articles

Bradford, Helen, 'Gentleman and Boers: Afrikaner nationalism, gender and colonial warfare in the South African War' (UNISA Library Conference 3–5 August 1998).

Kessler, Stowell, 'The black and coloured concentration camps of the South African War, 1899–1902: Shifting the paradigm from sole martyrdom to mutual suffering' (UNISA Library Conference 3–5 August 1998).

Mbenga, Bernard, 'The Bakgatla's role in the South African War and its impact on the Pilansberg, 1899–1903' (UNISA Library Conference 3–5 August 1998).

van Heyningen, Elizabeth, 'Women and disease – The clash of medical cultures in the concentration camps of the South African War' (UNISA Library Conference 3–5 August 1998).

Unpublished Diaries and Letters

Thomas Cook courtesy of Lady Treitel.

Diary of Nurse Ina Cowan courtesy of the Mafeking Museum.

James Cowland courtesy of Fred Simmons.

William Croome courtesy of Marcus Croome.

Percy Day courtesy of Daphne Seigal.

John Moody Lane courtesy of William Lane.

Alec Kearsey courtesy of Nick Fox.

Matthew Kelly courtesy of Joan Harrison.

Andrew MacKillop courtesy of Brian Jewell.

John Paterson courtesy of Elizabeth Warneford-Thompson.

Colin Pritchard courtesy of MCC Pritchard.

Will Saxon courtesy of Alan Wilson.

Mother Mary Stanislaus' Journal of the Siege of Mafeking courtesy of the Mafeking Museum.

Walker Henderson Thompson courtesy of Joan Thompson.

Bombadier Weeks courtesy of Cynthia Dize.

Jack Wynn courtesy of Richard Eccles and Peter Tinker.

Index

Page numbers in italics refer to captions and illustrations.

Tabitha Jackson's Acknowledgements

Assuming that no-one reads the acknowledgements section except to look for their own name, I hope this short list does not disappoint or neglect anyone who will be in a position to give me a job in the near future.

Thanks must go to Emma Tait for her infinite patience as my editor; Professor Fransjohan Pretorius for reading my manuscript and preventing me from making many embarrassing errors, although I take full responsibility for any that may remain; my friends and family for indulging my complete self-absorption, and especially Dinah Lord who went above and beyond the call of duty as a drinking companion; Liz Manson for excising many of the grosser pomposities from my manuscript and the production team at Twenty Twenty, in particular Jonathan Lewis, for giving me the opportunity to immerse myself in such a fascinating and important period of history.

Twenty Twenty Television's Acknowledgements

Twenty Twenty Television would like to thank the production team: Christine Anderson, Janette Ballard, Peter Eason, Victoria English, Laura Govett, Zita Hardy, Isobel Hinshelwood, Jim Howlett, Pearlie Joubert, Margaret Kelly, Alison McAllen, Claire McFall, Nadia McLeod, Claudia Milne, Julia La Rocha Miranda, Laura Noyce, Bea O'Connell, Musa Radabe, Bea Roberts, Simon Rockell, Michael Sanders, Alexander Sparks, Barret Stanboulian and Melanie Vasey. They would like to thank the historical consultants on the series: Bernard Mbenga, Thomas Pakenham, Fransjohan Pretorius and Iain Smith; and Fiona Barbour, Temba Buthelezi, Joe Dlamini, Ian and Lynn Fordred, Belinda Gordon, Albert Grundlingh, Johan Hatingh, Steve Lunderstedt, Bhekie Ntonbela and Liz Spiret.

Picture credits

While every effort has been made to trace copyright holders for photographs and illustrations featured in this book, the publishers will be glad to make proper acknowledgements in future editions in the event that any regrettable omissions have occurred at the time of going to press.

1: Greenwall Collection; 2/3: South African Library, Capetown; 4/5: Museum Africa; 6: Greenwall Collection; 7: Cape Town Archives; 8: National Maritime Museum/E.T. Archive (painting by Willaerts); 12: KwaZulu-Natal Provincial Museum Service Collections; 13: National Archives of South Africa; 14 Consolidated Goldfields/E.T. Archive (painting by Sir Luke Fildes); 14: Museum Africa; 15: Museum Africa; 16: Museum Africa; 17: Greenwall Collection; 20: Greenwall Collection; 21: Greenwall Collection; 22(t): War Museum of the Boer Republics, Bloemfontein; 22(b): Museum Africa; 23: National Archives of South Africa, Pretoria; 24: Domenica del Corriere/E.T. Archive; 25: Greenwall Collection; 27: National Cultural History Museum, Pretoria; 28: Greenwall Collection; 29: Greenwall Collection; 30: War Museum of the Boer Republics, Bloemfontein; 31: War Museum of the Boer Republics, Bloemfontein; 32: ML Design; 33: Cape Town Archives; 34/5: Elleanor Cason (photograph by David Taylor); 36/7: Mitchell Library, Sydney/E.T. Archive; 38/9: Museum Africa; 40: McGregor Museum, Kimberley; 40: Elleanor Cason (photograph by David Taylor); 44(t): Janice Farquharson; 44(b): Greenwall Collection; 45: Greenwall Collection; 46: Dr R. Greenwall; 48: National Cultural History Museum, Pretoria; 49(t): War Museum of the Boer Republics, Bloemfontein; 49(b): Greenwall Collection; 50: National Cultural History Museum, Pretoria; 52: War Museum of the Boer Republics, Bloemfontein; 53: Cape Town Archives; 54/5: War Museum of the Boer Republics, Bloemfontein; 57: Dr R, Greenwall; 58: National Archives of South Africa, Pretoria; 59: William Lane; 60: McGregor Museum, Kimberley; 61: Greenwall Collection; 62: War Museum of the Boer Republics, Bloemfontein; 64(t): Greenwall Collection; 64(b): Greenwall Collection; 65: Dr R. Greenwall; 66: Greenwall Collection; 68: Greenwall Collection; 70/1: Pietermaritzburg Archives Repository; 72(l): War Museum of the Boer Republics, Bloemfontein; 72(r): Alexander Thorneycroft/KwaZulu-Natal Provincial Museum Service Collections; 73: ML Design; 74: KwaZulu-Natal Provincial Museum Service Collections; 76: War Museum of the Boer Republics, Bloemfontein; 77: National Archives of South Africa; 78: National Cultural History Museum, Pretoria; 79: Ladysmith Siege Museum; 80: Arnold van Dyk; 81: War Museum of the Boer Republics, Bloemfontein; 82: Talana Museum, Dundee; 83: KwaZulu-Natal Provincial Museum Service Collections; 84: Greenwall Collection; 85: Greenwall Collection; 86: Arnold van Dyk; 88: Cape Town Archives/Barnet Collection; 89: Greenwall Collection; 90: National Archives of Canada/McGregor Museum, Kimberley; 91: War Museum of the Boer Republics, Bloemfontein; 92: Museum Africa; 94: Talana Museum, Dundee; 94/5: Talana Museum, Dundee; 96: E.T. Archive; 97: Domenica del Corriere/E.T. Archive; 98/9: Pietermaritzburg Archives Repository; 100/1: War Museum of the Boer Republics, Bloemfontein; 102: Greenwall Collection; 105: Museum Africa; 107: Mafeking Museum; 108(l): Mafeking Museum; 108(r): Elleanor Cason (photograph by David Taylor); 109: Greenwall Collection; 110: John and Benmie Bottomley; 111: KwaZulu-Natal Provincial Museum Service Collections; 112(t): Greenwall Collection; 112(b): Greenwall Collection; 115: War Museum of the Boer Republics, Bloemfontein; 116/7: National Cultural History Museum, Pretoria; 118: Arnold van Dyk; 120/1: Graaff-Reinet Museum; 123: South African National Museum of Military History; 125: Arnold van Dyk; 126: South African Library, Capetown; 127: Greenwall Collection; 128/9: Pietermaritzburg Archives Repository; 130: Biebe van der Merwe; 132(t): War Museum of the Boer Republics, Bloemfontein; 132(b): Greenwall Collection; 133: Richard Eccles/Peter Tinker; 134: War Museum of the Boer Republics, Bloemfontein; 137: Philip Tucker; 138/9: Cape Town Archives; 140: Greenwall Collection; 141(l): Greenwall Collection; 141(r): Greenwall Collection; 142: Museum Africa; 143: Greenwall Collection; 144: Cape Town Archives; 146: Graaff-Reinet Museum; 147: Museum Africa; 148/9: War Museum of the Boer Republics, Bloemfontein; 150: Greenwall Collection; 151(l): Richard Eccles/Peter Tinker; 151(r): National Archives of South Africa, Pretoria; 152: Greenwall Collection; 153(l): Greenwall Collection; 153(r): War Museum of the Boer Republics, Bloemfontein; 154: Talana Museum, Dundee; 155: War Museum of the Boer Republics, Bloemfontein; 156: War Museum of the Boer Republics, Bloemfontein; 157: War Museum of the Boer Republics, Bloemfontein; 159: Vereeniging Museum; 161: National Archives of South Africa, Pretoria; 163: Kay de Villiers; 164: National Archives of South Africa, Pretoria; 165: War Museum of the Boer Republics, Bloemfontein; 166: Philip Tucker; 167: War Museum of the Boer Republics, Bloemfontein; 169: Greenwall Collection; 170: War Museum of the Boer Republics, Bloemfontein; 172: Museum Africa; 174: War Museum of the Boer Republics, Bloemfontein; 175: War Museum of the Boer Republics, Bloemfontein; 176: Greenwall Collection; 178: National Cultural History Museum, Pretoria; 179: Graaff-Reinet Museum; 180: War Museum of the Boer Republics, Bloemfontein; 181: Greenwall Collection; 182/3: Free State Provincial Archives, Bloemfontein; 185: Greenwall Collection; 186: National Cultural History Museum, Pretoria.